Aliaksandr Sukhanevich

The Japanese Cruiser Asama

KAGERO

Portside view.

Programme 6 + 6

The victorious war against China in 1895 had a bittersweet taste for Japan. The intervention of three world powers (Russia, Germany and France) deprived it of territorial gains. At the same time, Japan realized the maritime weakness of the Land of the Rising Sun in relation to the West. The Japanese did not accept the status of a poor relative and decided to join the rivalry in the field of naval armaments. In the second half of 1895, a 10-year fleet expansion programme was passed in parliament. Its implementation was to bring Japan into the first league of maritime powers. The construction of six battleships and four armored cruisers has become a priority. After some analyzing, the Japanese concluded that six battleships might not be enough to defeat the main enemy they thought Russia was. As the budget was insufficient to build additional battleships, in 1897 the number of armored cruisers was increased to six. The latter built at that time were well armored and heavily armed. This new type of cruiser was superior to many of the older battleships. The fleet command found these ships a valuable addition to the line fleet. Thus, the 6 + 6 Programme was born.

"Asama" was one of the six armored cruisers built under the programme. Four of them were built by the British Armstrong shipyard, but "Asama" was ordered in France, and its sister vessel, the "Yakumo", in Germany. Both cruisers were to carry British guns, making them compatible with units built in hazy Albion. The contract for the construction of "Asama" was signed on 12th of October, 1897, with Ateliers et Chantiers de la Loire. On 1st of February, 1898, the keel was laid at the concern's shipyard in St. Nazaire. The launch took place on 24th of June, 1899. The construction was completed on 28th of July, 1900. The next day, the cruiser left St. Nazaire and went to Japan, reaching Yokosuka on 29th of October 29 of that year.

Design

The prototype for the Japanese cruisers was the "O'Higgins" cruiser, built at that time by the English for the Chilean fleet. The basic design of all six Programme's cruisers was essentially the same: 8 inch main caliber artillery, side armor along the entire length of the hull, and a speed of 20–21 knots. Due to the weakness of their own shipbuilding industry, the construction of cruisers was commissioned to foreign shipyards (four in England, one in France and one in Germany). Each shipyard had a certain freedom to modify the details of the design. In the case of "Asama", the famous French designer Amable Lagane used a long narrow hull with a not too high freeboard and two main artillery turrets, one at the bow and stern. The attempt to combine two different philosophies of building cruisers: the English and the French, turned out to be unsuccessful. Instead of a super cruiser, "Asama" became the worst of the six. The ship's power plant, equipped with Belleville boilers (considered technically advanced), were quite unreliable. The main innovation was the use of a forced draft device on the chimneys, which allowed simultaneous air intake

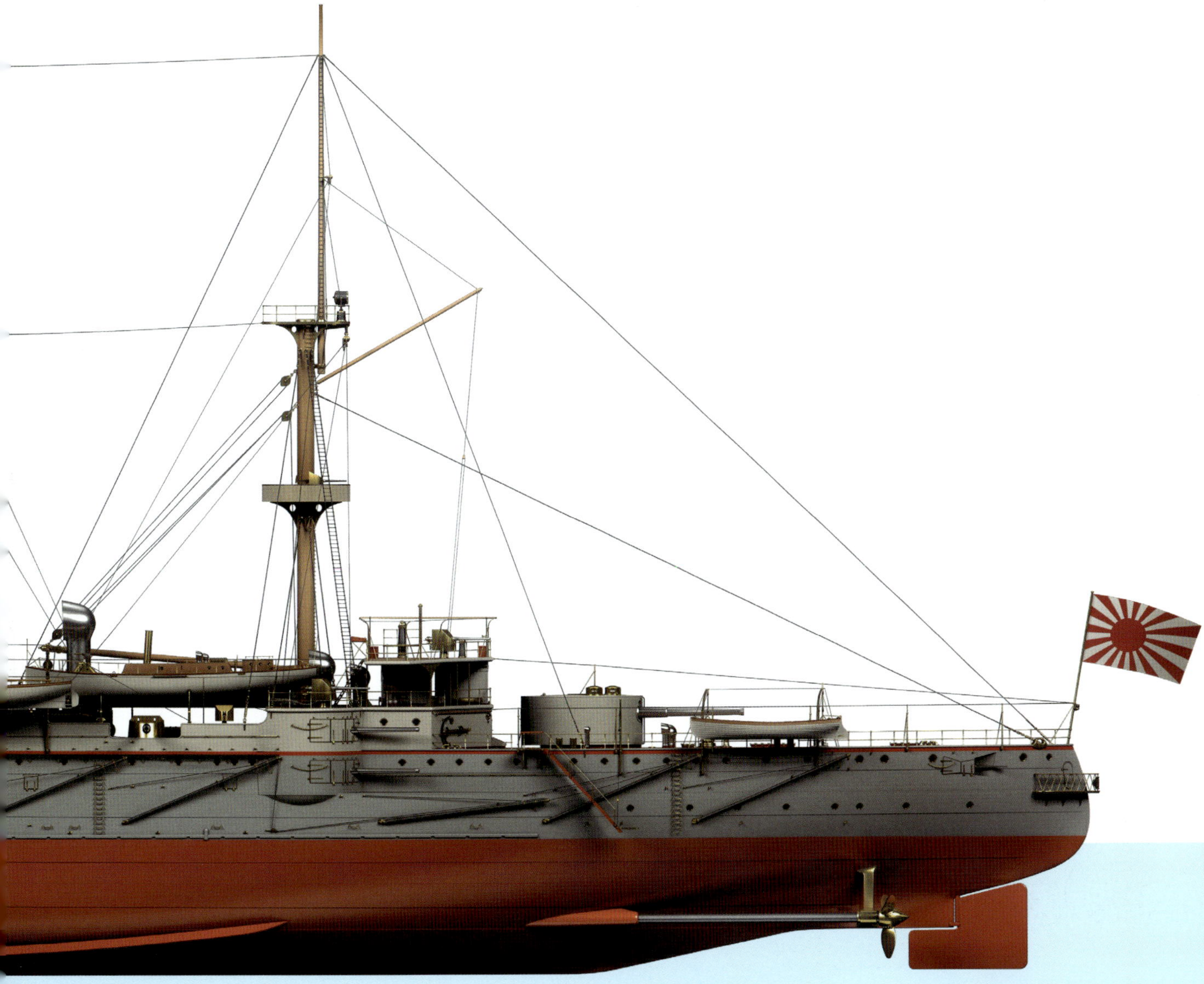

and smoke extraction. Modern British and German ships used a separate air intake, which turned out to be a problem during combat, as these devices, along with the air, also drew smoke and debris into the engine room.

Construction

The smooth-deck hull, with a slight saddle of the upper deck and a slight collapse of the side in the amidships area, was made of mild steel in a mixed system. The bow (similar to the stern) was made of steel with a slightly forward underwater part (ram type). The cruiser's hull was separated by 12 transverse bulkheads into 13 watertight compartments. A long hull with a length to width ratio of 7.3:1, combined with a traditional rudder (instead of a semi-balanced one) made maneuvering quite difficult. At the same time, it was a problem for the Imperial Navy due to the lack of a dry dock of the appropriate length. Moving the bow artillery turret maximally towards the bow, together with the lack of a typical half-shell, made the ship "wet", i.e. exposed to frequent flooding of the fore deck. The cruiser had a characteristic three-funnel silhouette, and it differed from a similar "Yakumo" by a larger gap between the second and third funnels. This was due to the fact that the bow and stern groups of boilers were separated by an intermediate compartment. In line with British tradition, the machine compartments were placed aft, which allowed for a rational arrangement of medium-caliber artillery ammunition chambers.

Armament

The main armament of the "Asama" was four 203 mm/45 (8 inch) Armstrong type 41 naval guns, housed in two twin armored turrets. The firing sector of both turrets was around 250 degrees. The angle of raising the barrels was from -5 to +15 degrees (according to other data up to +30°) ensured a maximum range of 18.000 meters. The fire unit was 80 rounds per gun and was smaller than on the other units of the programme (120 rounds), due to the fact that the entire ammunition was placed in the chambers under the armored deck, which in turn were smaller due to the shift with the turrets towards the narrower ends of the hull. Each tower had two elevators: one for carrying projectiles, the other for gunpowder charges. The auxiliary artillery battery consisted of 12 152 mm/40 (QF 6 inch) Armstrong guns, eight of which were placed in casemates and four were placed on the upper deck, covered with masks. The angle of raising the barrels was from -7 to +15 degrees. The range was 9140 meters, and the rate of fire was 5–6 shots per minute. The fire unit was 120 (150) rounds per gun. Each of the guns had its own individual elevator for feeding ammunition of a separate type.

For defense against torpedo boats ship had twelve 76 mm guns (12-pound QF 12 cwt) and eight 47 mm (QF 3-pound) caliber Hotchkiss guns. Four 76 mm guns were placed on the roof of the upper 152 mm gun casemates, another four in unarmored casemates below the upper deck at the fore and aft, and the remaining four on the sides amidships, alternating with 152 mm guns. Two of the 47 mm guns were placed on masts on platforms, and the rest on superstructures.

Starboard view.

Top view.

The latter could be placed on steam boats. "Asama" was also armed with five 457 mm (18 inch) fixed torpedo tubes, one (surface) launcher was located in the bow, and four other were placed underwater, two on each side.

Armor

The main side armor belt stretched along the entire length of the hull. It was 178 mm thick at amidships and decreased to 89 mm at bow and aft sections. The side armor was 213 cm high, of which 150 cm was under water. The upper armor belt was 127 mm thick and extended from the upper edge of the main side belt to the upper deck. Its length was 61.49 m. In the fore part it ended on a 76 mm thick traverse closing the citadel from the front. The barbets of the main caliber artillery turrets had armor thickness of 152 mm. The main artillery towers and the front of the casemates were protected by 152 mm thick armor. The sides and back of the casemates were protected by 51 mm thick armor plates. The remaining four guns had 76 mm thick protective masks in the forehead section. The armored deck, made of mild nickel steel, was 51 mm and 63 mm on slants. The armor plates of 127 mm thickness and above that

were made of cemented Krupp steel, the thinner ones were made of nickel steel.

Engine room

The cruiser was powered by two 4-cylinder triple-expansion steam engines with a total indicated power of 17.000 KM. Steam for the machines was supplied by 24 Belleville steam boilers. Design speed was 21 knots. The stock of 1,275 tons of coal provided a swim range of 7.000 NM at a speed of 10 knots. The machines were not distinguished by reliability, and the main reason for this was the low build quality. Belleville boilers tended to leak steam under high pressure.

Service history

A few years after entering service, "Asama" took part in the Russo-Japanese War (1904–1905). Baptism of fire took place on 9th of February, 1904, in the pending battle of the Japanese Combined Fleet with the Russian Pacific Squadron at Port Arthur. "Asama" suffered minor damage in battle. Until the end of February, she stayed in the area

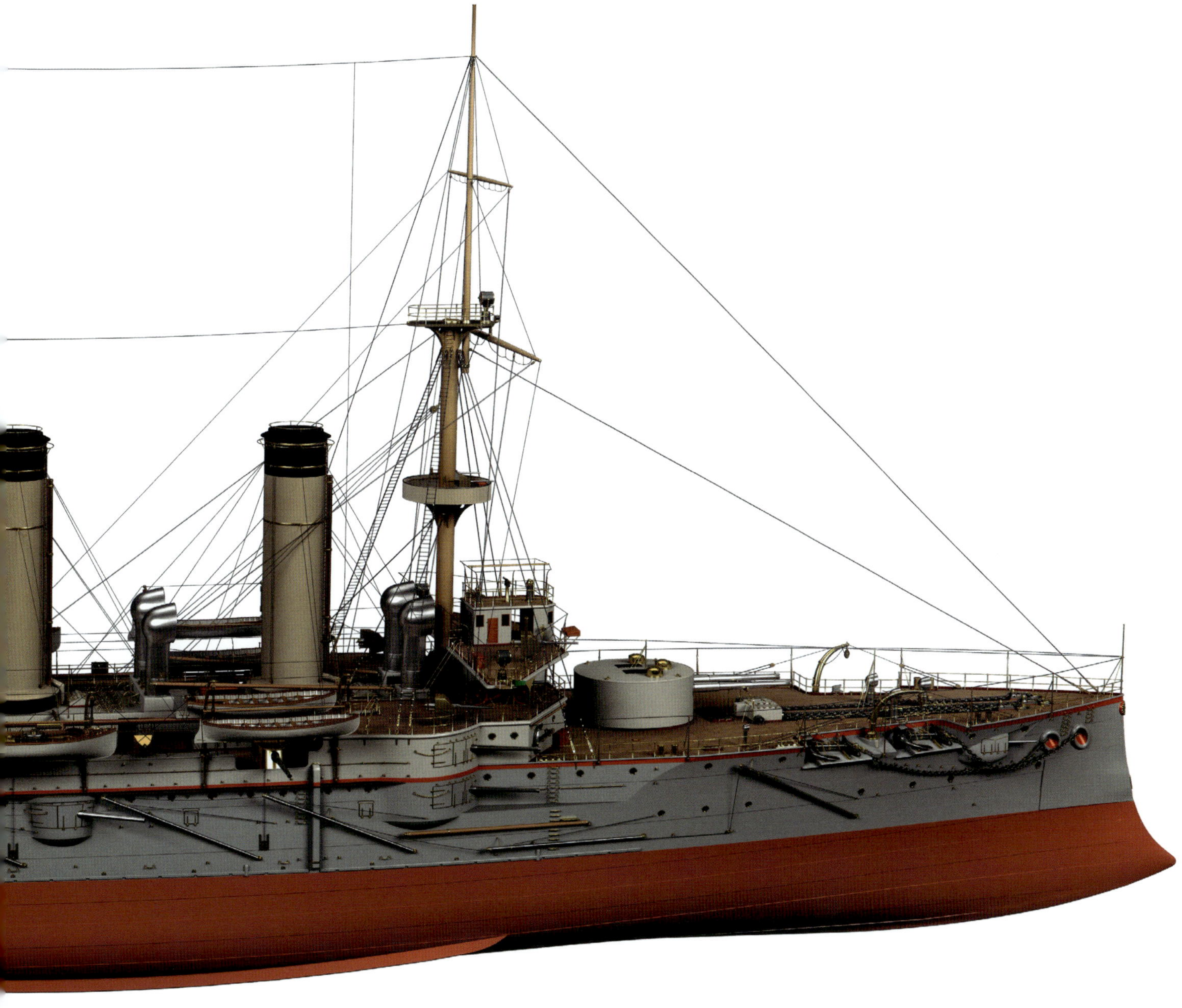

Overall view of the ship, starboard side.

of Arthur's Port, taking part in minor skirmishes with Russian ships. On 14th of August, 1904, the Japanese task force with "Asama" in its composition managed to intercept Russian ships, leading to the Battle of Ulsan. "Asama" sank the Russian cruiser "Rurik" and damaged two others. She suffered ten hits itself; eight crew members were injured. At the beginning of February 1905 it was repaired. During the renovation, platforms for light guns were removed from masts (to improve the cruiser stability). On 27th of May, 1905, the Battle of Tsushima took place. The artillery duels with Russian ships damaged, among others, one 203 mm and one 152 mm aft gun, as well as a rudder, forcing the cruiser to retreat from the battlefield. Ten crew members were killed and 30 were injured.

On 20th of April, 1912, "Asama" was assigned to the training squadron, cruising with cadets of the Imperial Naval Academy. She did not participate in World War I. After the end of the war, on 6th of June, 1920, "Asama" left the School Squadron. On 1st of September, 1921, she was reclassified as a 1st class coastal defense ship, although due to the poor condition of the mechanisms, she practically did not go to sea. On 8th of September, 1921, she became a stationary training ship of the Navy Corps in Maizuru. In 1924, it was partially disarmed, only four 203 mm, eight 152 mm, four 76 mm remained, also one AA 76 mm gun was added. Three torpedo tubes have been removed. On 1st of October, 1927, "Asama" was officially reclassified into a stationary training ship for the maritime engineering school in Maizuru. In 1941 she was completely disarmed and transformed into a hulk. On 15th of February, 1944, "Asama" was removed from the fleet list. On 18th of July, 1945, she was bombed and sunk by American Task Force 38 planes in Yokosuka. In 1946 "Asama" was scrapped.

Tactical and technical data

Displacement (standard tons): 9263 during tests, 9426 normal, 10.112 full;
Displacement (metric tons): 9411 during tests, 9577 normal, 10.274 full;
Dimensions: max. 138 (131.1 on water line/131.55 between perpendiculars) × 18.1 × 7.2–7.6 m;
Drive: 2 × VTE/RcLoire, 24 Belleville boilers (working steam pressure 20 kg/cm^2, grate area 112 m^2, heating area of the boilers 3578 m^2); power indicated in KM – 17.000 ihp at 20 knots; on tests 13.372 ihp at 19.9 knots;
Range: 3900 Mm at 10.5 knots;
Coal supply: 600/1275 ts;
Armament: 2 × 2 – 203/40, 12 – 152/40, 12 – 76/40, 8 – 47/40, 5 457 mm torpedo tubes;

Armor:
- side: 178–127–89 mm,
- deck: 51 mm (slants 63 mm),
- traverses: 76 mm,
- main artillery: 152 mm,
- barbets: 152 mm,
- 152 mm gun casemates: 51 mm,
- command post: 356 mm (roof 51 mm),
- auxiliary command post: 76 mm.

Table No. 1. Distribution of the masses

Item	Mass in tonnes	%
Hull and equipment	3 665	39.5
Armor	2 459	28.5
Devices and systems	427	4.6
Armament	919	9.9
Machines and boilers	1 206	13.0
Normal coal stock	603	6.5
Normal displacement	9 278	100

Table No. 2. Artillery characteristics

Caliber of the gun, mm	203	152	76	47
Type/model	Pattern U/ Type 41	Pattern Z/ Type 41	Type 41	Mle 1885
Project/Producer	Elswick/Armstrong	Elswick/Armstrong	Armstrong/ Kure	Hotchkiss
Barrel length, calibers	45	40	40	40
Barrel length, mm	10 170	6 324	3 124	2 049
Gun weight with lock, t	19.5	6,5	0.54	0.25
Lock type	piston	piston	piston	wedge
Projectile/payload weight, kg	95.3/113.4*/25	45.4/8.3	5.7/0.9	1.6/0.13
Muzzle velocity, m/s	859/787*	762	647	562
Fire range, m/cables	18 000/65	9 140/55	7 400/40	3 700/20
Rate of fire, rounds per minute	3	6	10	20

* For heavy projectile.

Overall view of the ship, port side.

Bow view.

Stern view.

View of the bow of the ship, starboard side.

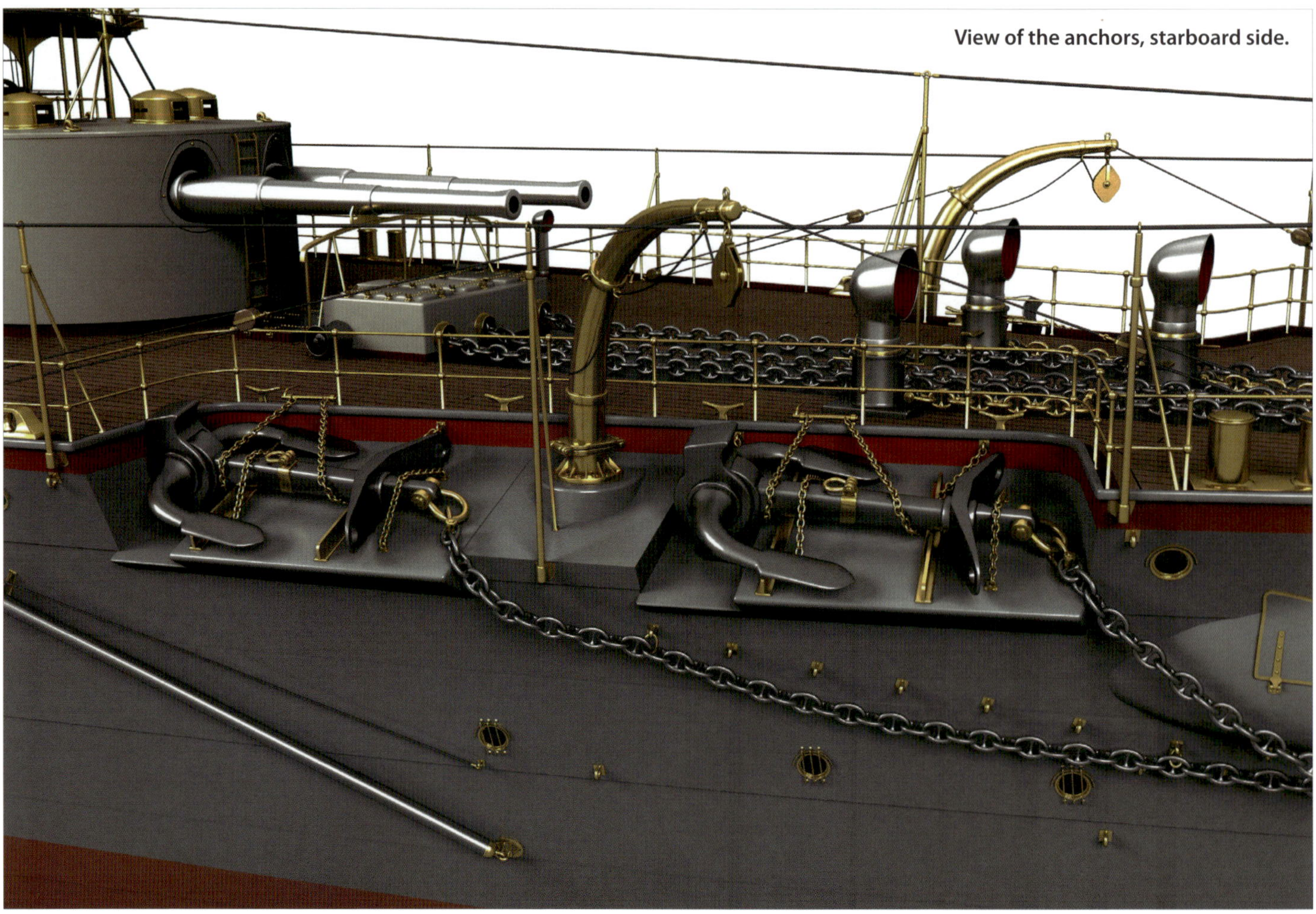
View of the anchors, starboard side.

View of the forward superstructure and the 6-inch gun turret, starboard side.

View of the bow sponsons of the 6-inch guns, starboard side.

View of the deck mounting of the 6-inch gun, starboard side.

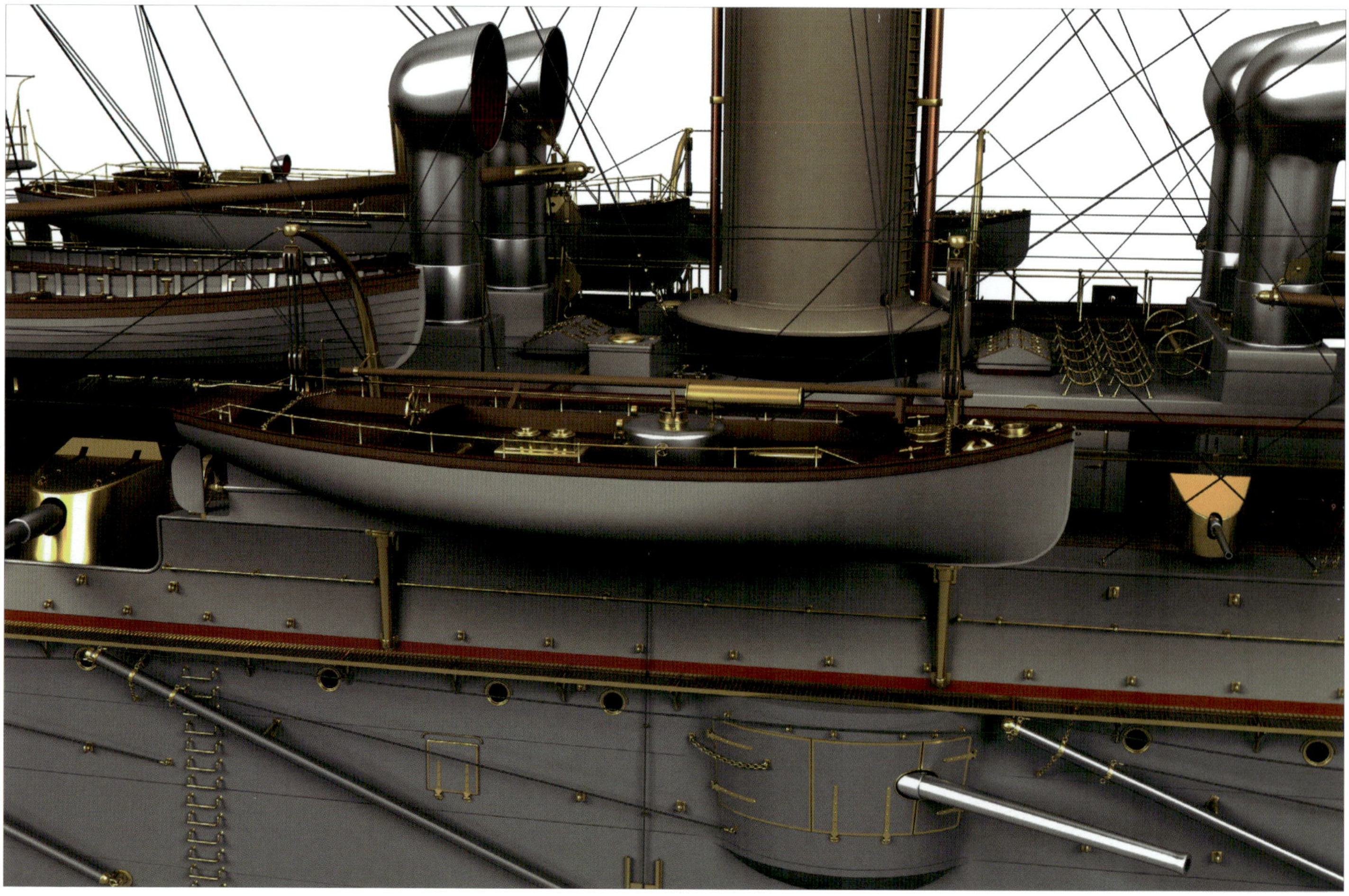
View of the steam boat, starboard side.

View of the stern sponsons of the 6-inch guns, starboard side.

View ofthe stern bridge, starboard side.

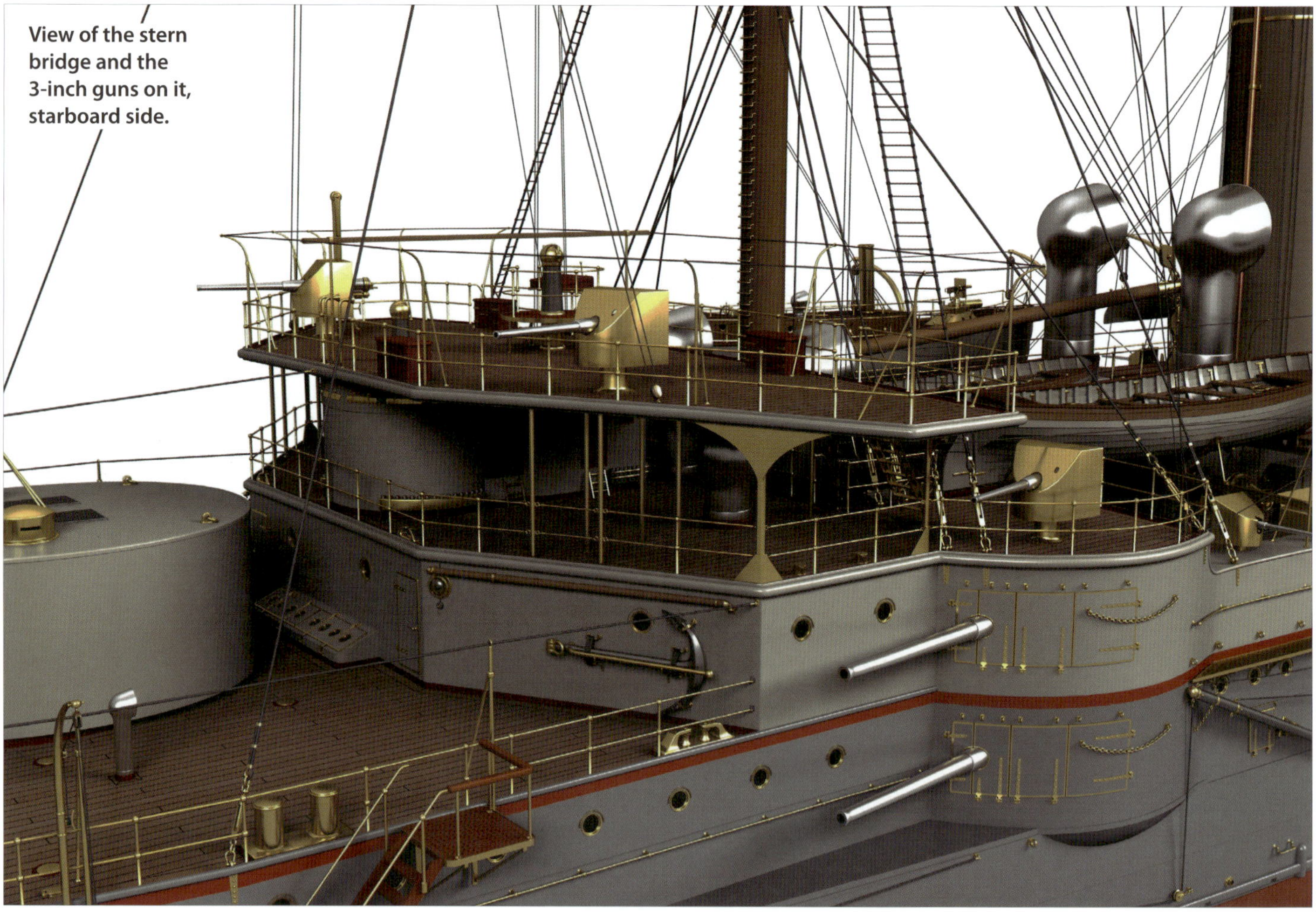

View of the stern bridge and the 3-inch guns on it, starboard side.

View of the ramp, starboard side.

View of the stern balcony.

View of the stern balcony.

View of the stern turret of the 8-inch guns, starboard side.

View of the stern superstructure, starboard side.

View of the stern bridge.

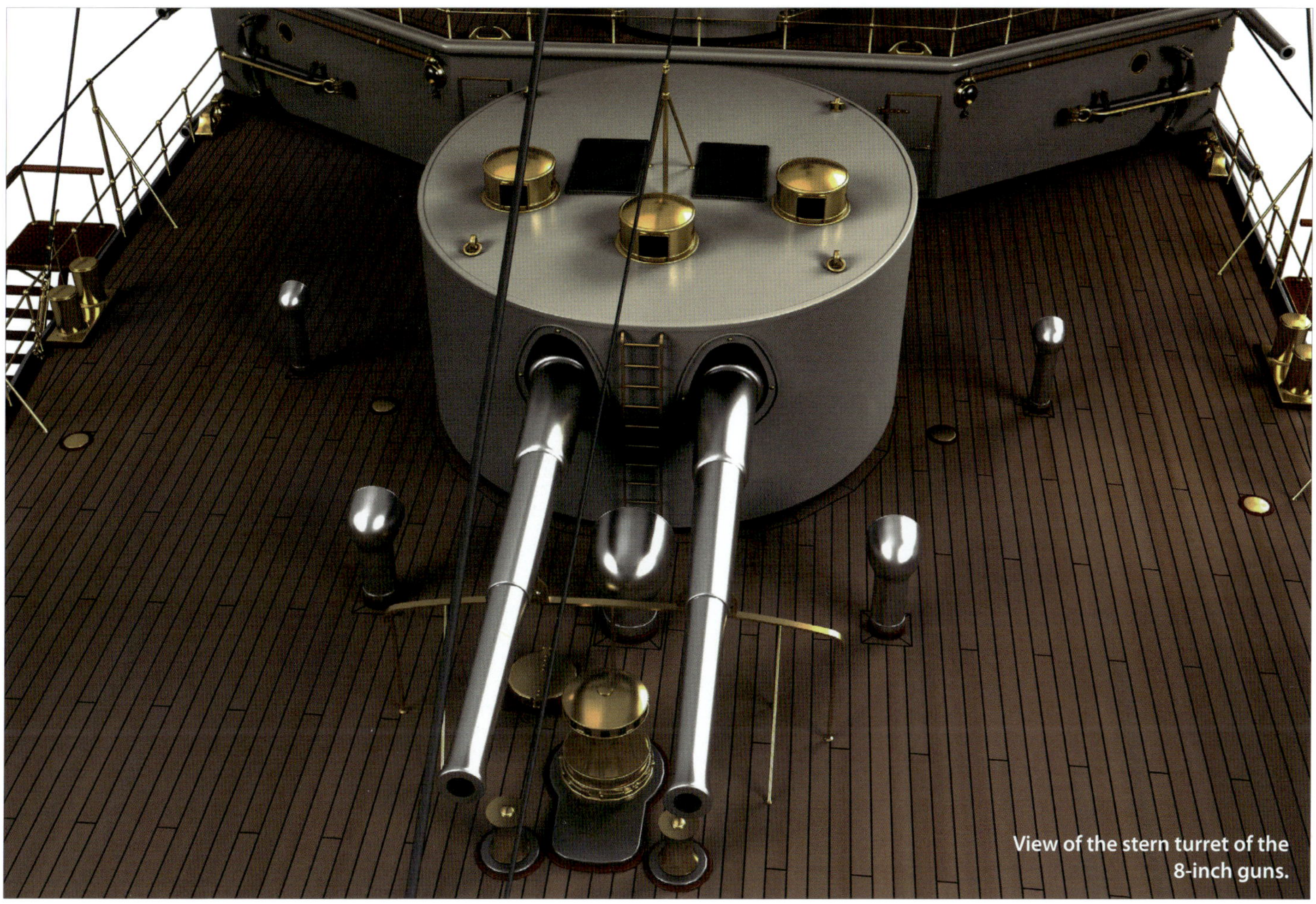

View of the stern turret of the 8-inch guns.

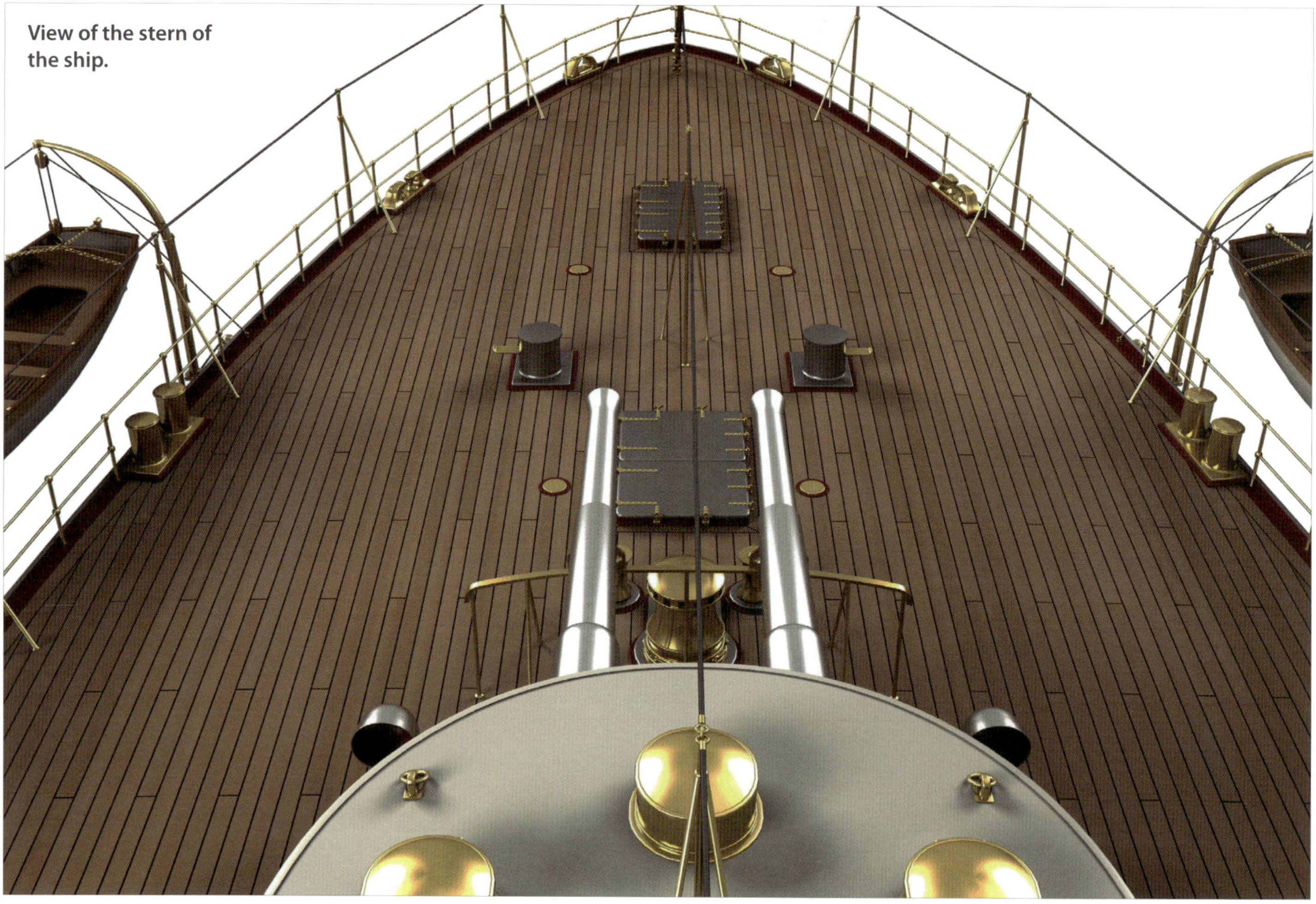

Overall view of the middle part of the ship, starboard side.

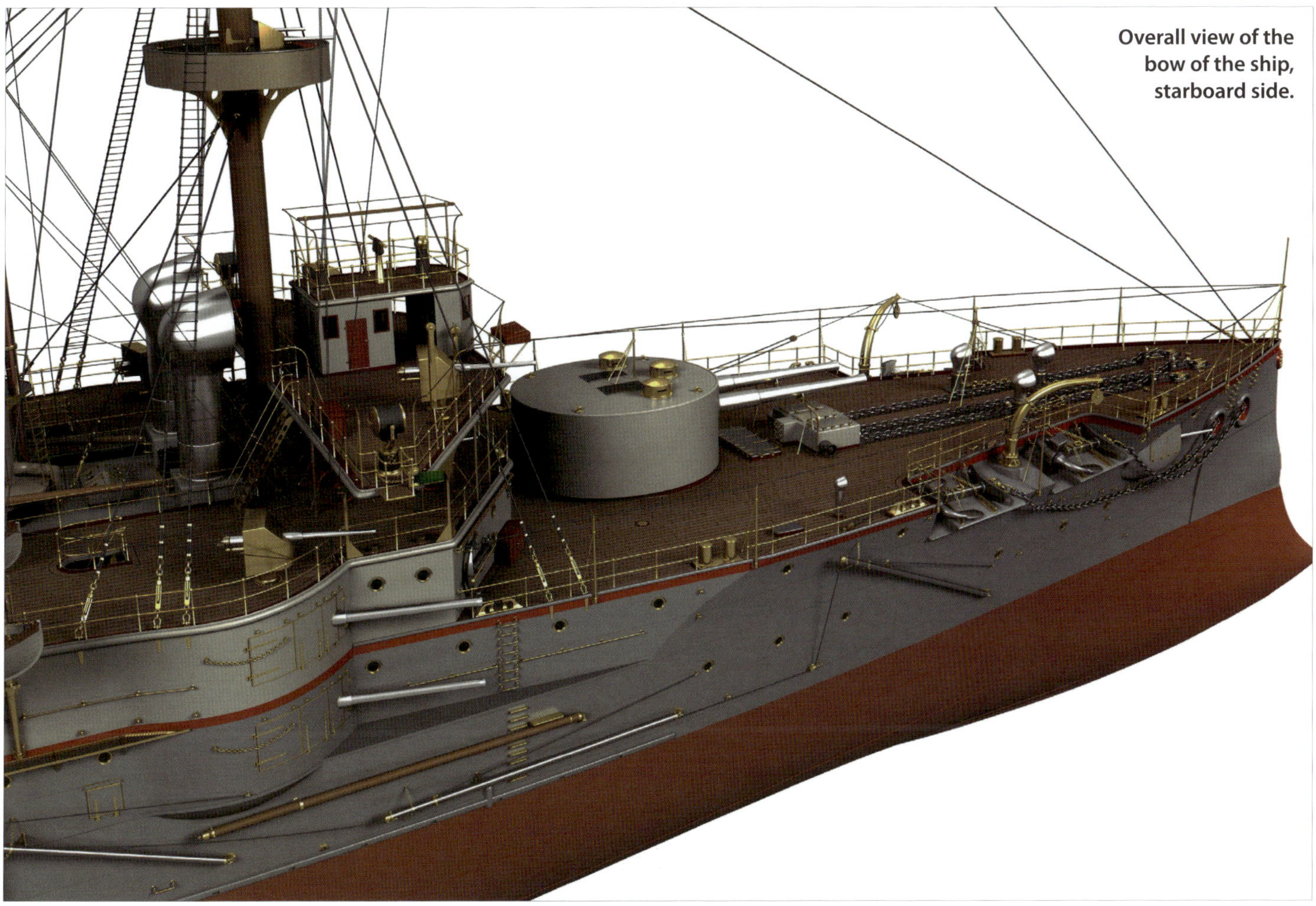

Overall view of the bow of the ship, starboard side.

Overall view of the bow of the ship, starboard side.

View of the bow bridge, starboard side.

View of the bow turret of the 8-inch guns.

View of the bow of the ship.

View of the bow superstructure, starboard side.

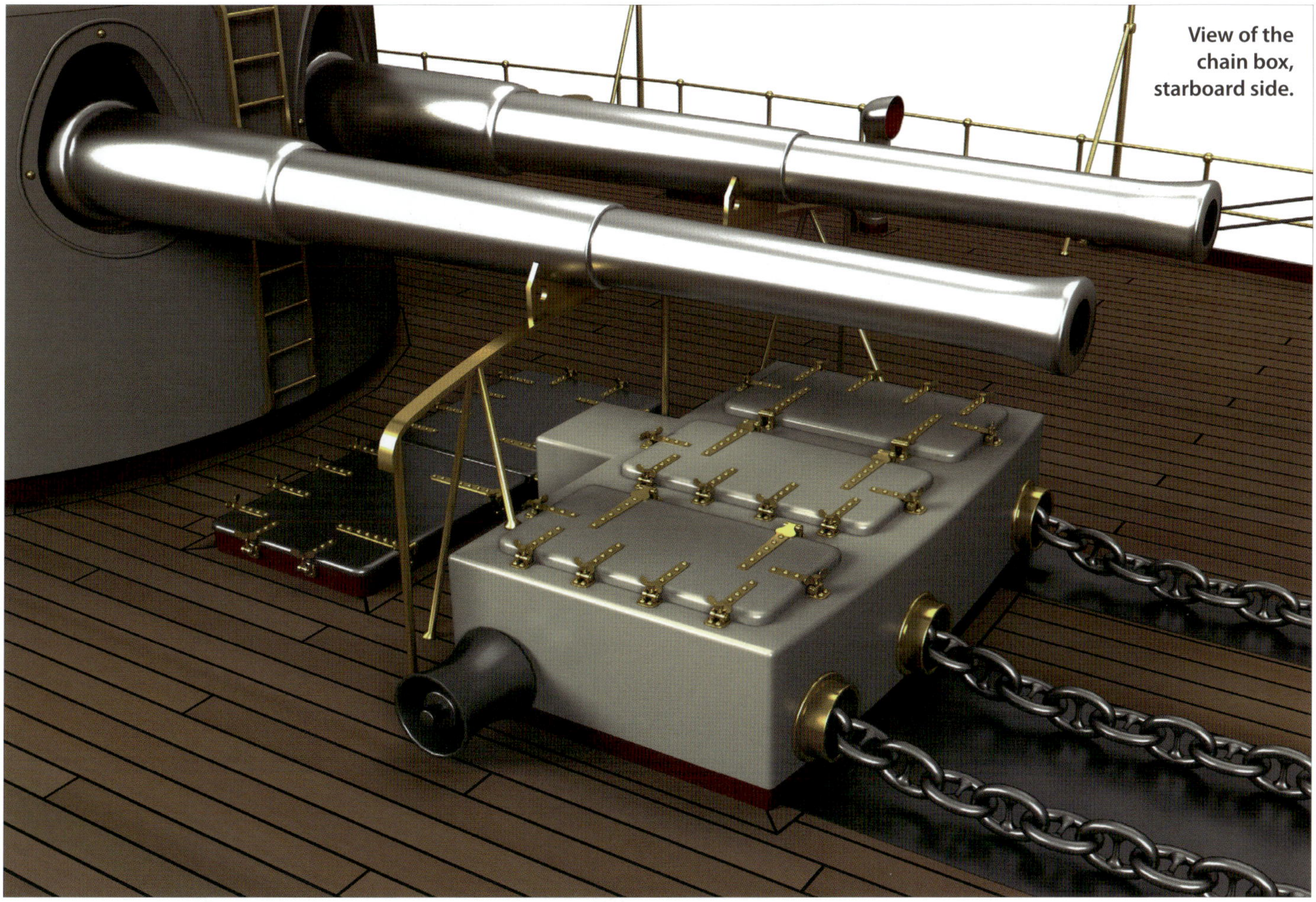

View of the chain box, starboard side.

View of the deck clews.

▲ Overall view of the funnel area, starboard side.

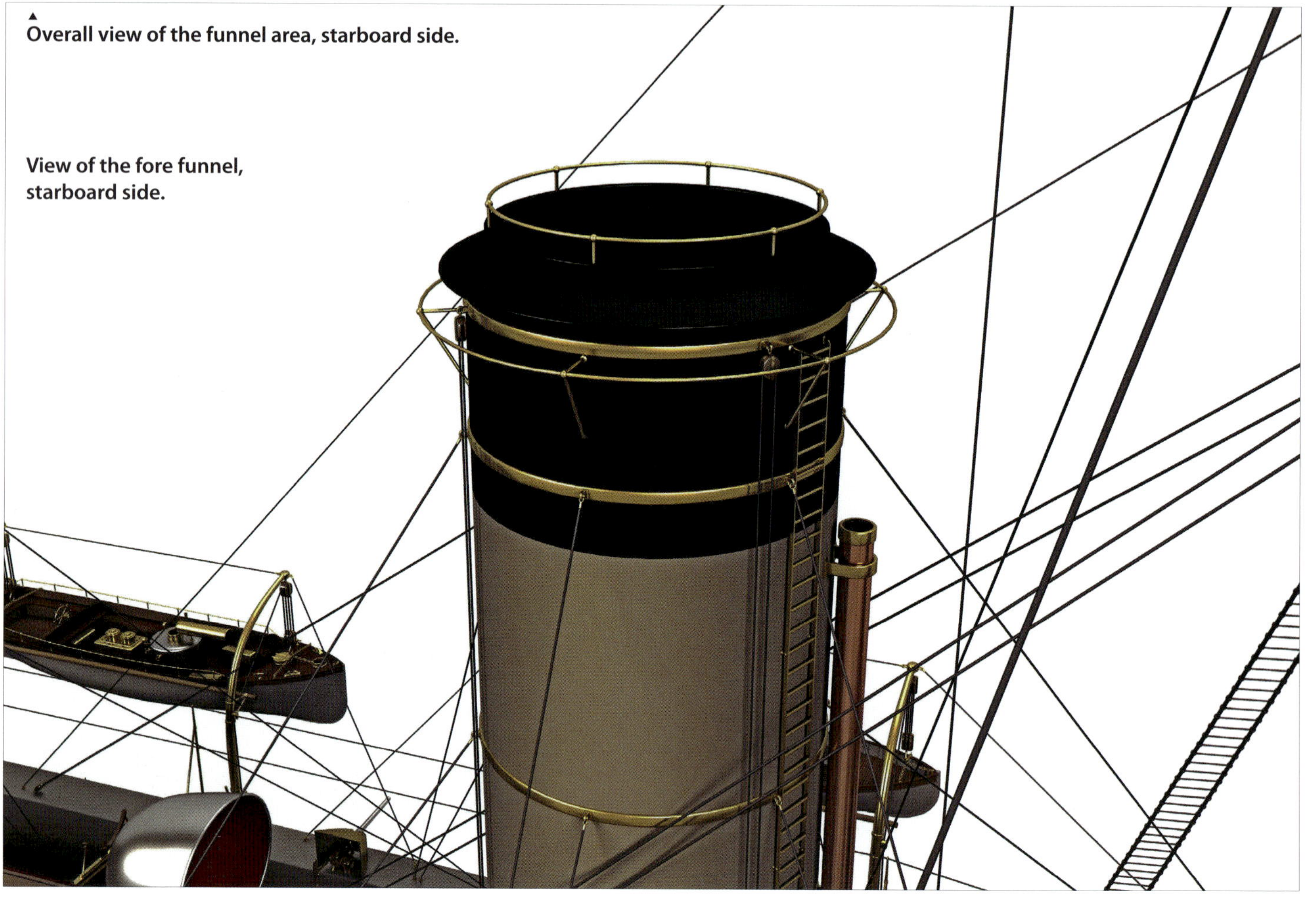

View of the fore funnel, starboard side.

Overall view of the central part of the ship, starboard side.

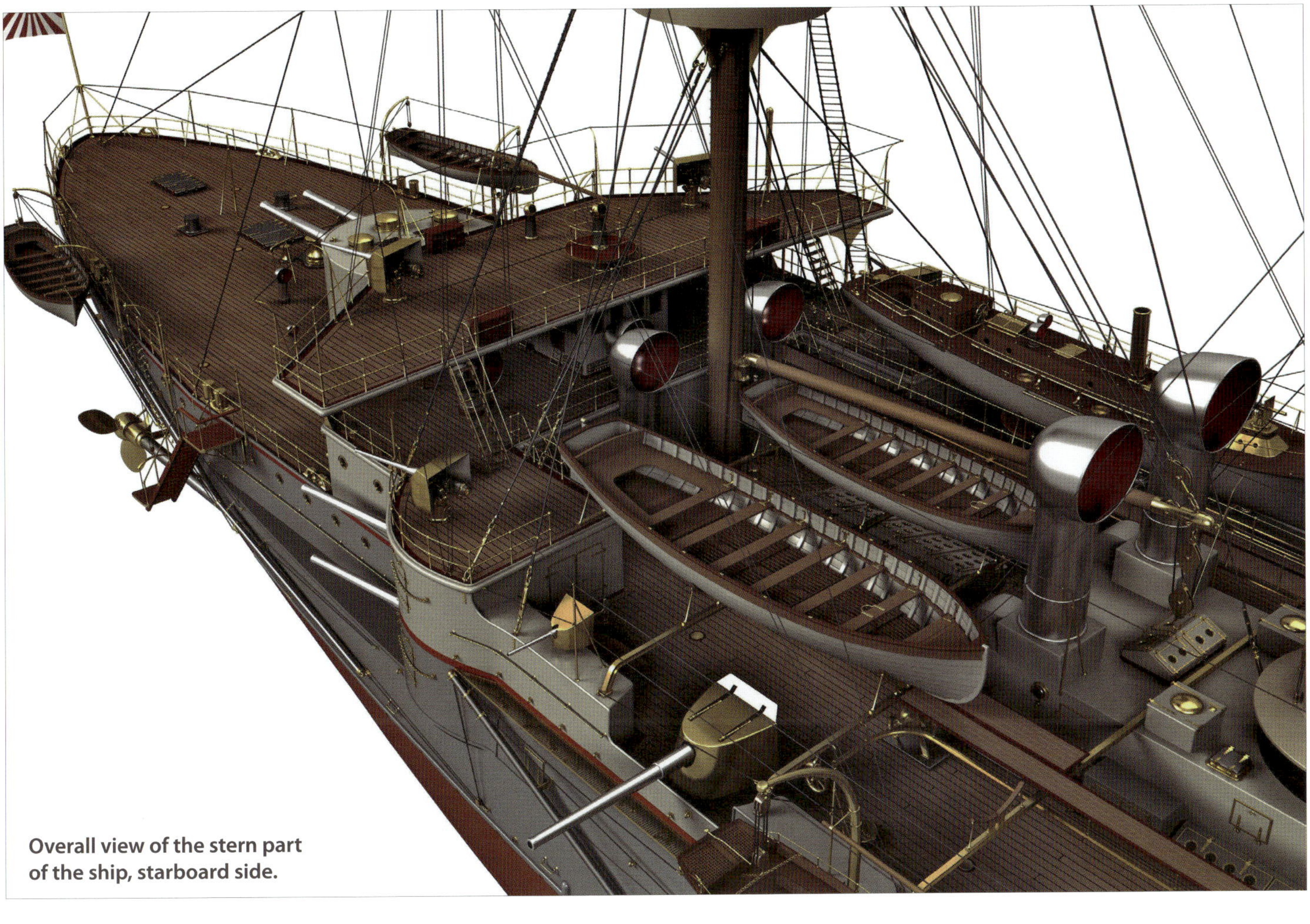

Overall view of the stern part of the ship, starboard side.

View of the topsail platform mainmast, starboard side.

View of the searchlight area of the mainmast, starboard side.

View of the searchlight platform mainmast, starboard side.

View of the topsail platform foremast, starboard side.

View of the bow bridge and 3-inch gun, starboard side.

12-pounder 8 cwt Armstrong gun (landing gun), starboard side.

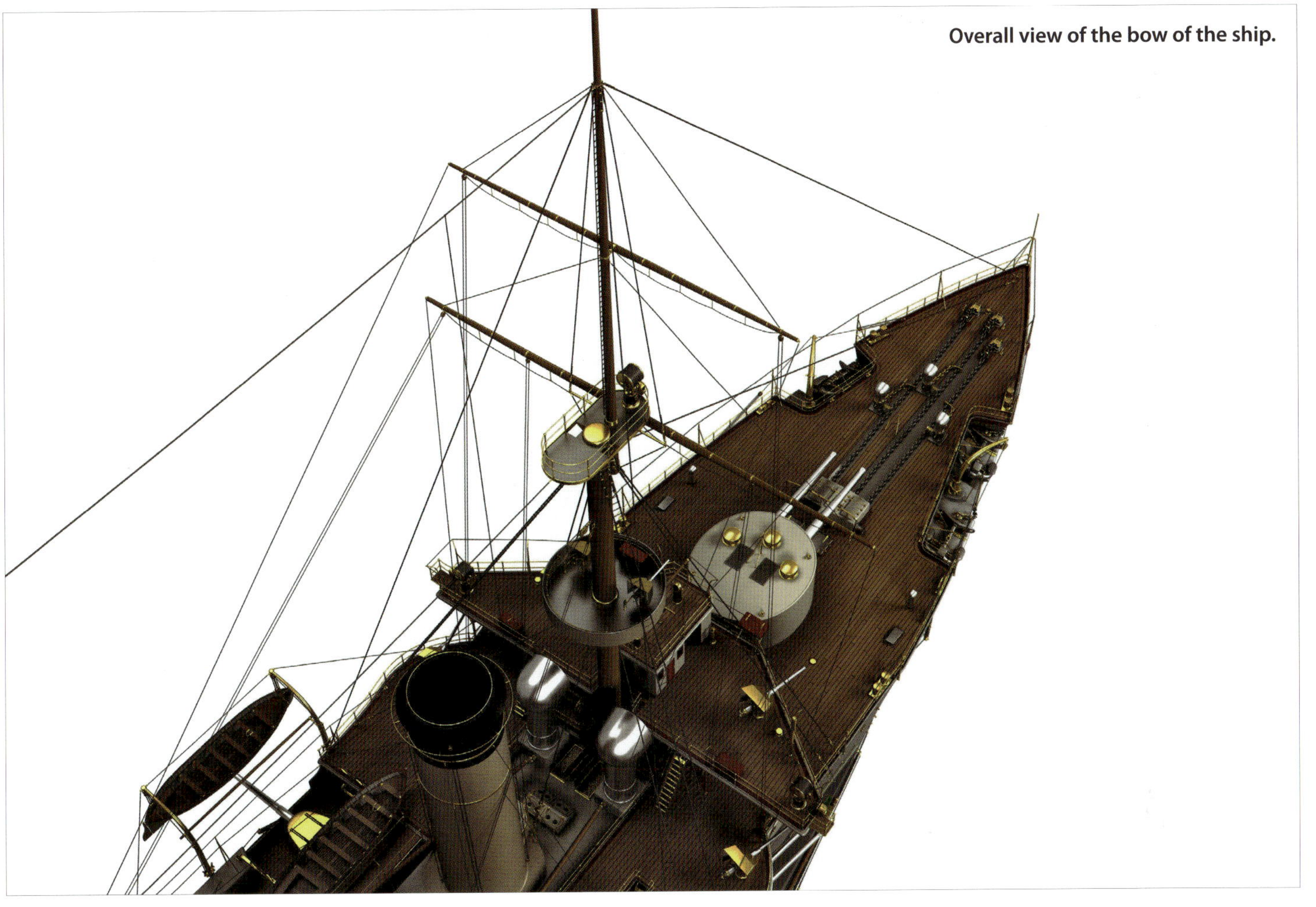

Overall view of the bow of the ship.

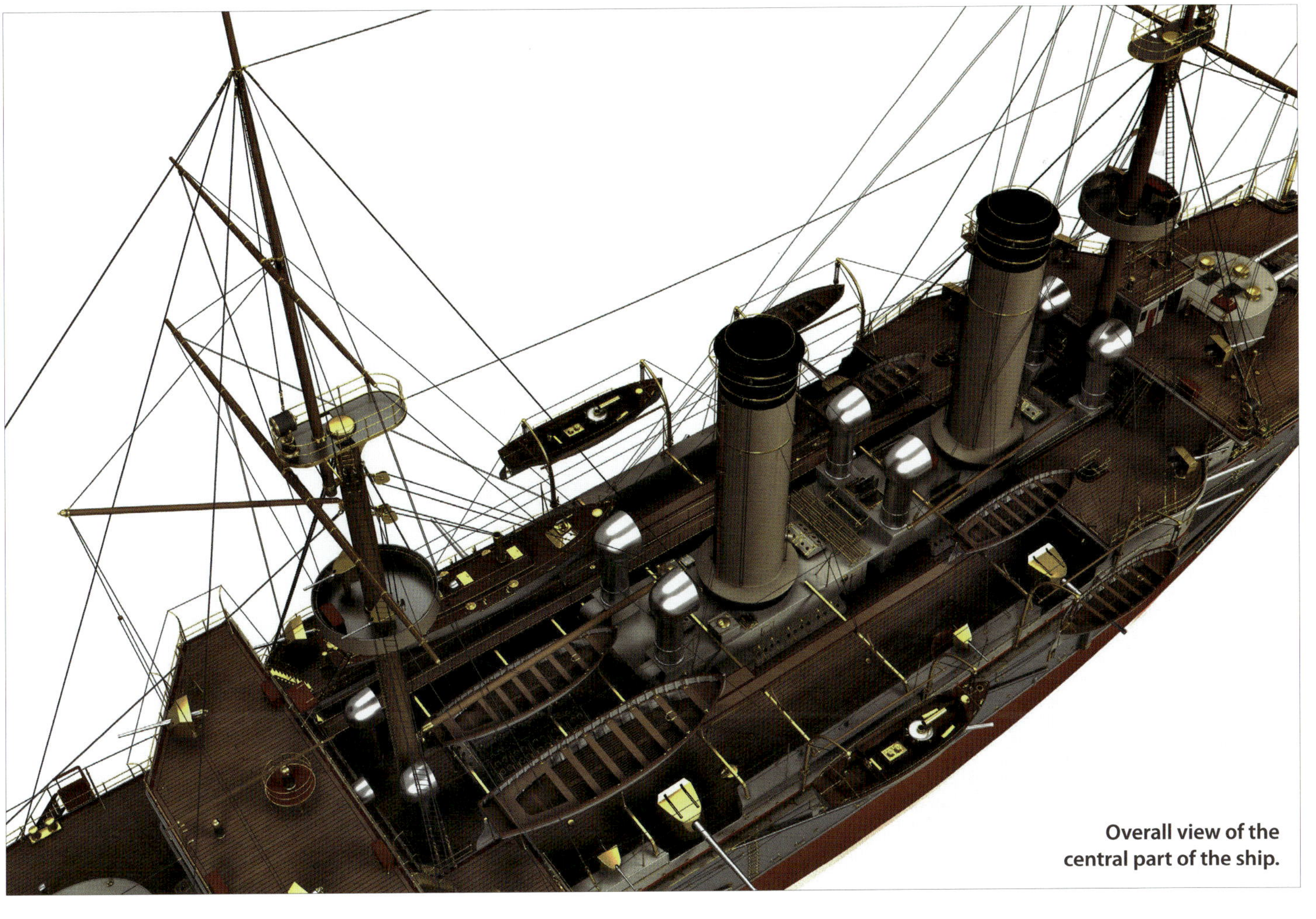

Overall view of the central part of the ship.

Overall view of the ship from starboard side

Overall view of the ship from port side

Overall view of the stern part of the ship.

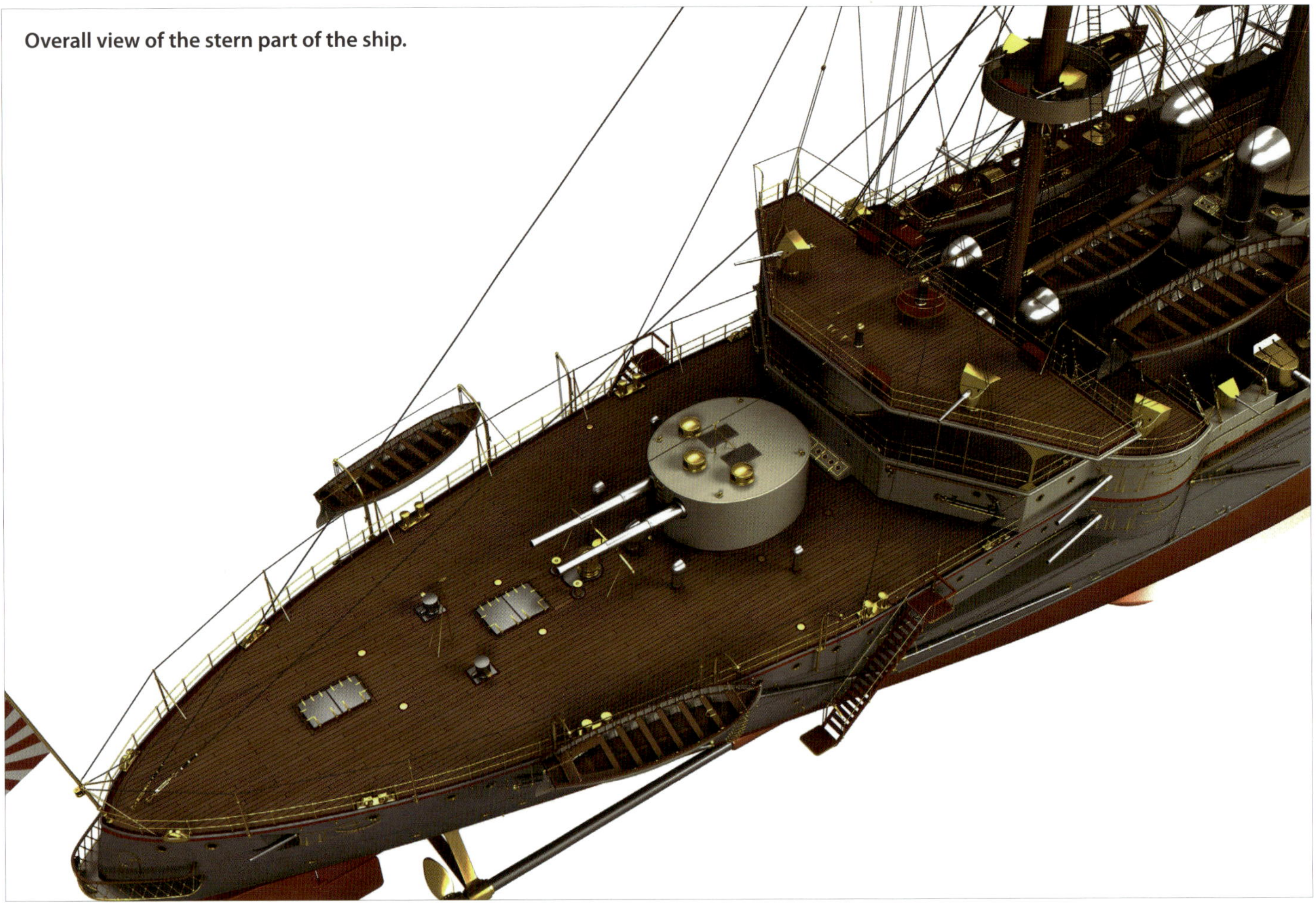

View of the starboard side of the ship.

View of the starboard side of the ship.

View of the starboard side of the ship.

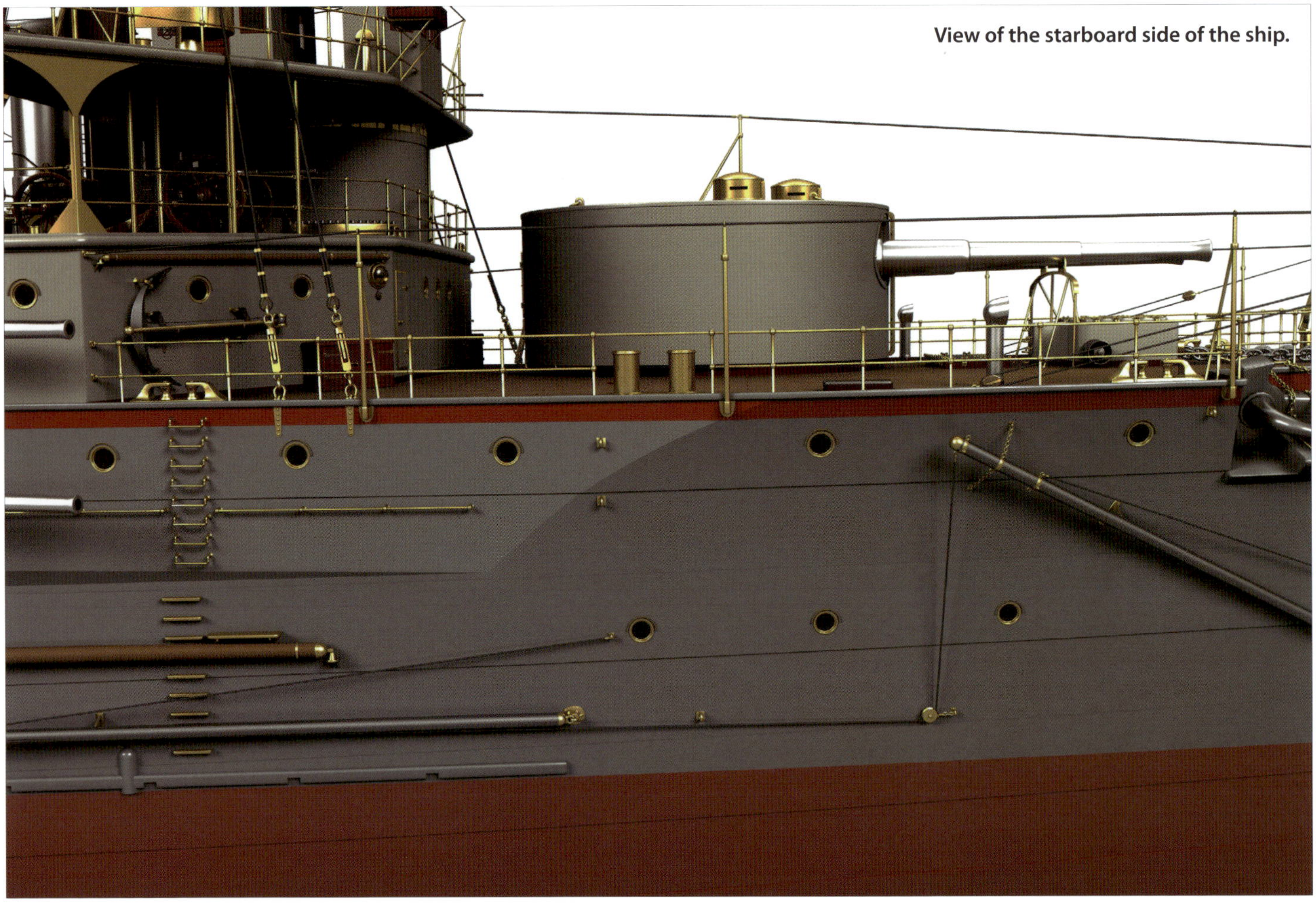

View of the starboard side of the ship.

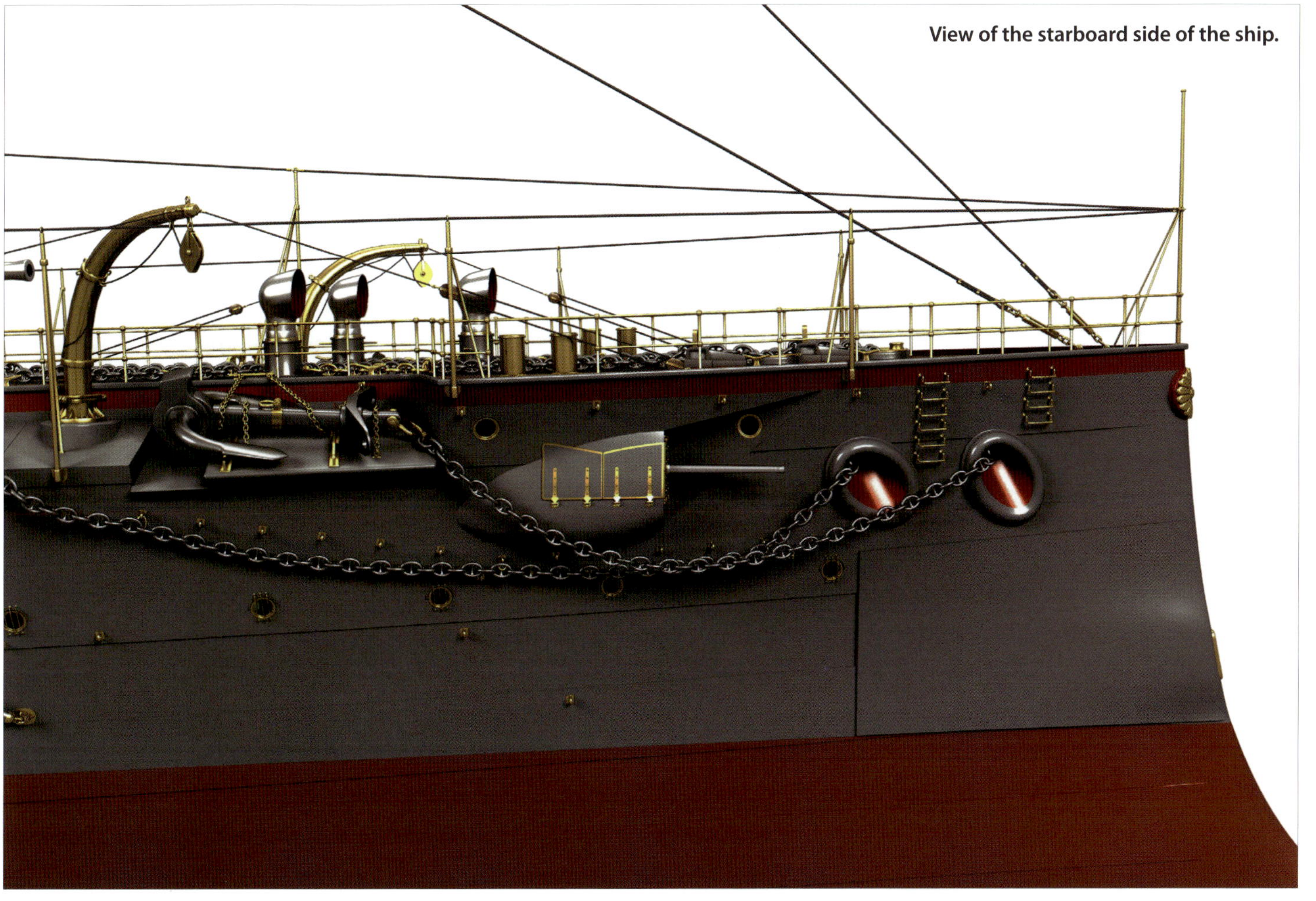
View of the starboard side of the ship.

View of the stern part of the ship, starboard side.

Overall view of the bow of the ship, starboard side.

Overall view of the bow of the ship, port side.

View of the deck 6-inch gun, starboard side.

View of the ventilation pipes, starboard side.

View of the bow sponsons of the 6-inch guns, starboard side.

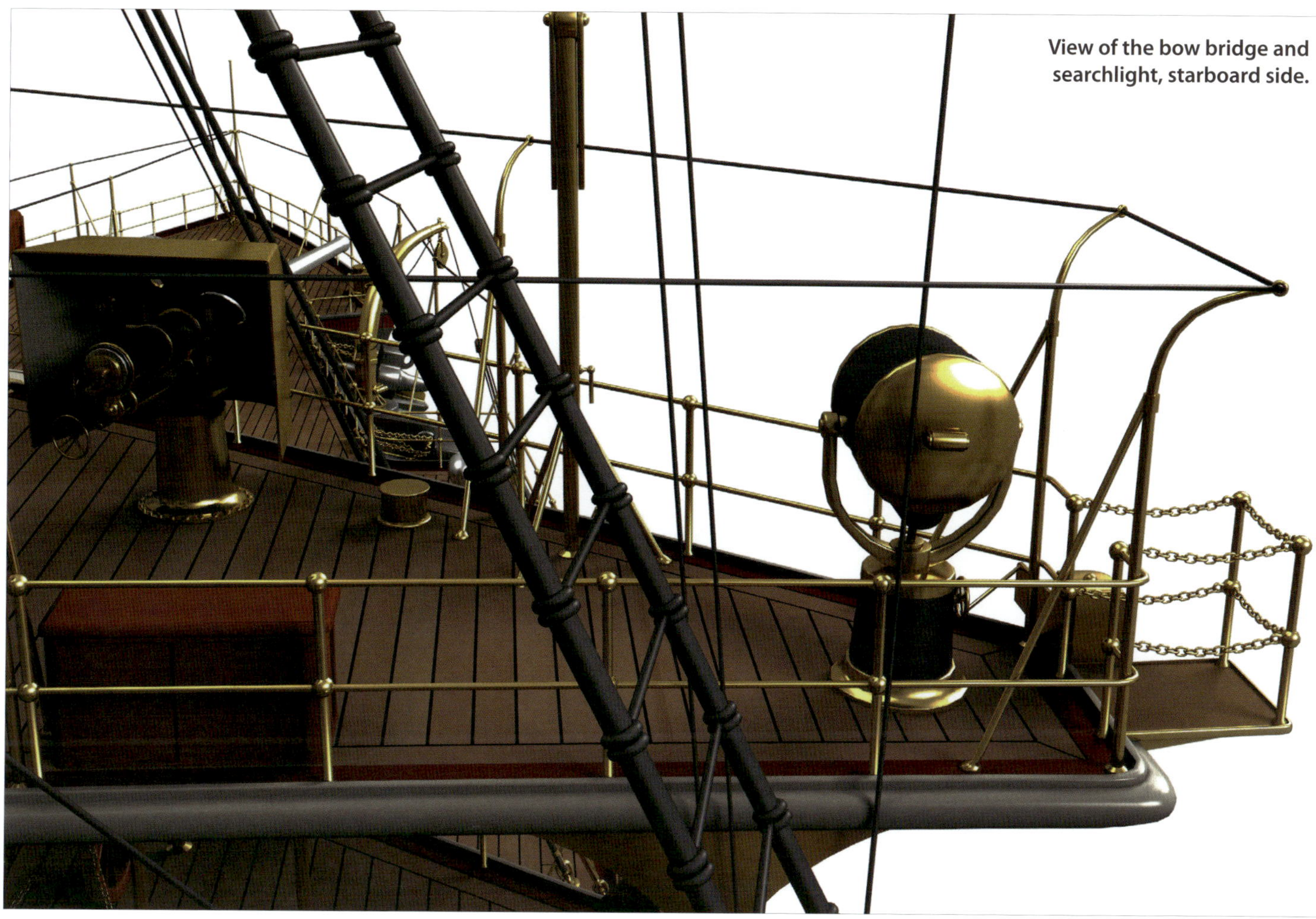

View of the bow bridge and searchlight, starboard side.

View of the central superstructure, starboard side.

View of the anchor, port side.

Overall view of the bow superstructure, port side.

Overall view of the central part of the ship, port side.

View of the steam torpedo boat, port side.

Overall view of the stern part of the ship, port side.

View of the steam torpedo boat, port side.

View of the stern deck 3-inch gun, port side.

View of the steam torpedo boat, port side.

View of the stern superstructure, starboard side.

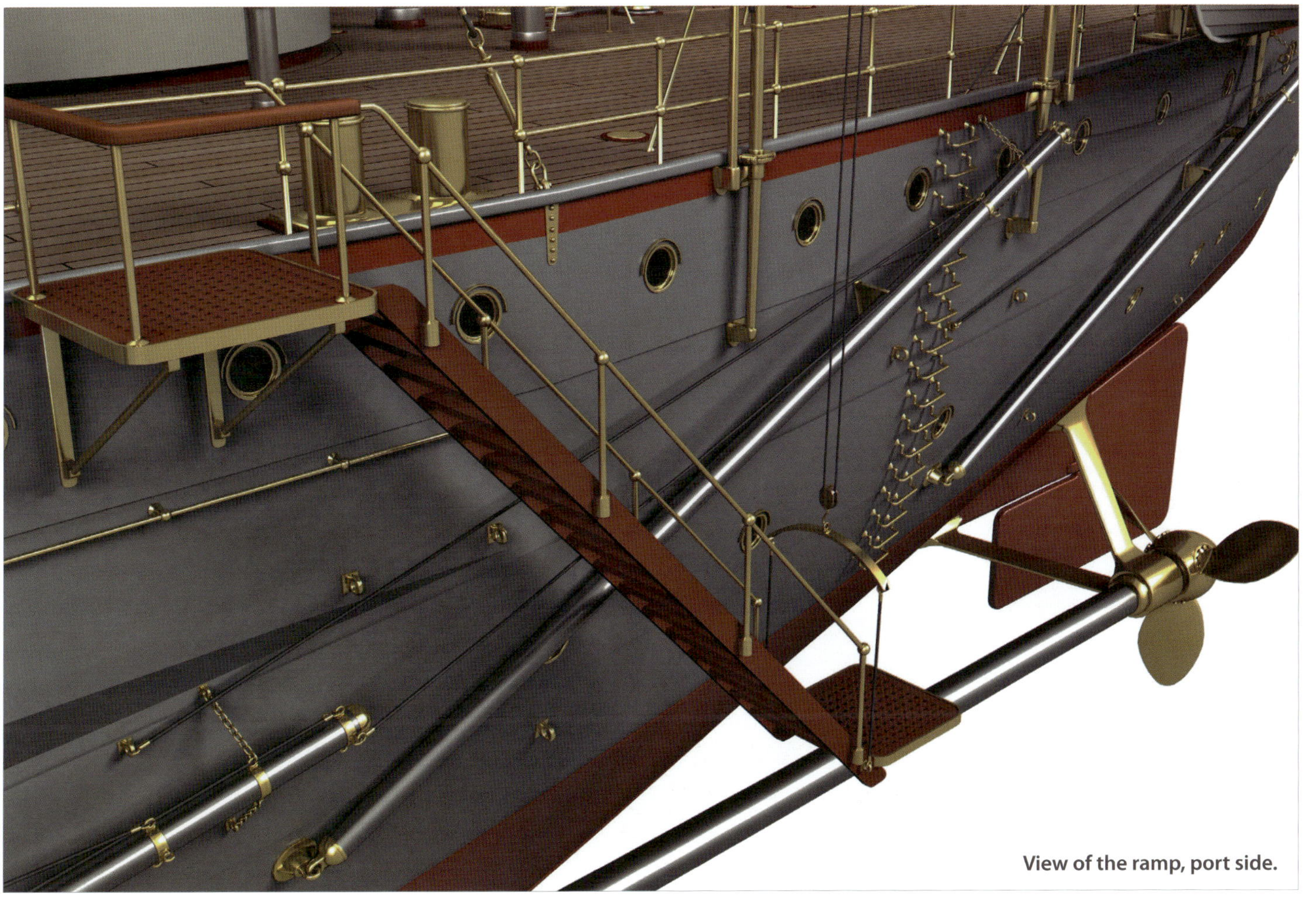

View of the ramp, port side.

View of the stern part of the ship, port side.

View of the bow bridge, port side.

View of the fore funnel, port side.

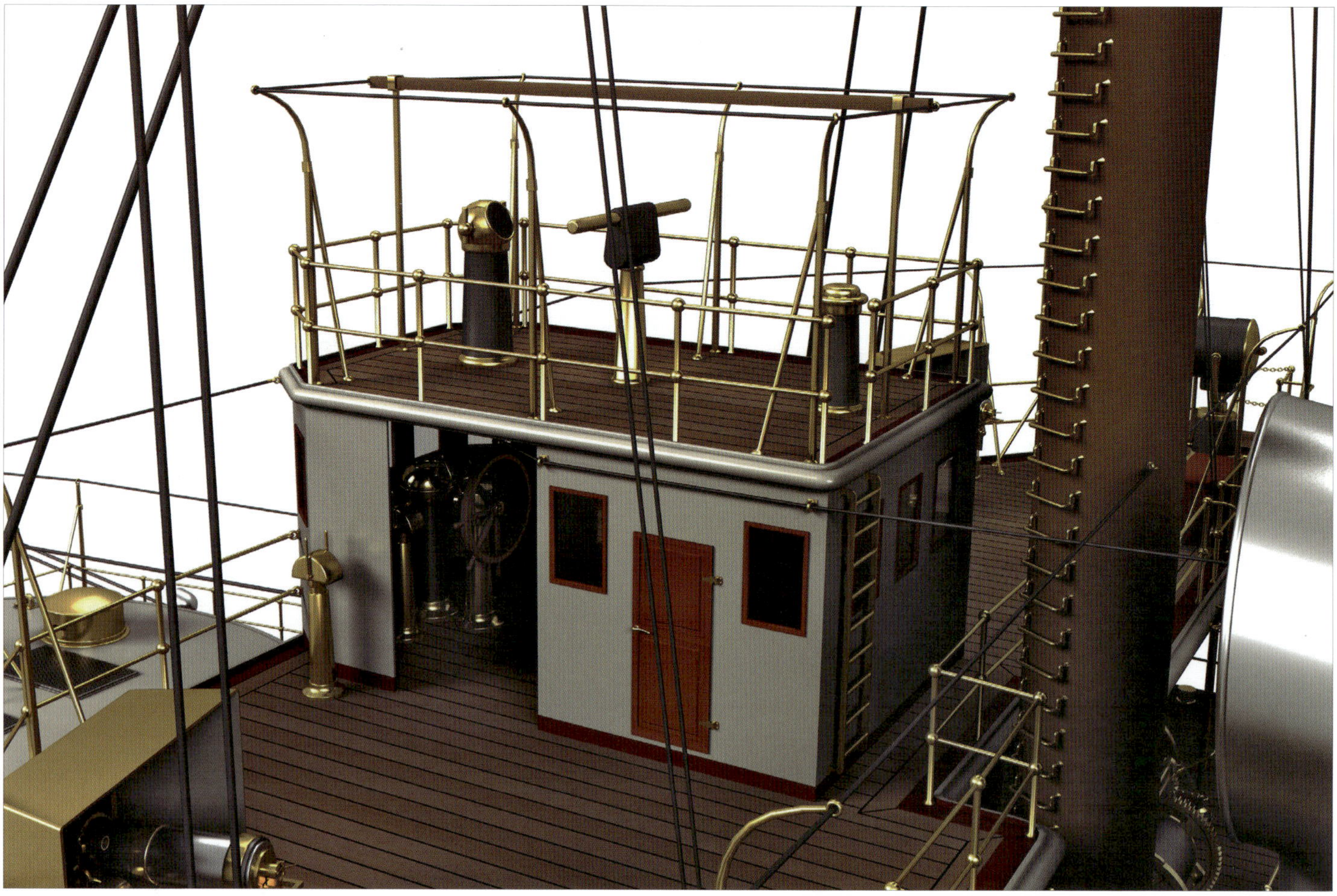

View of the chart room, port side.

View of the chain box, port side.

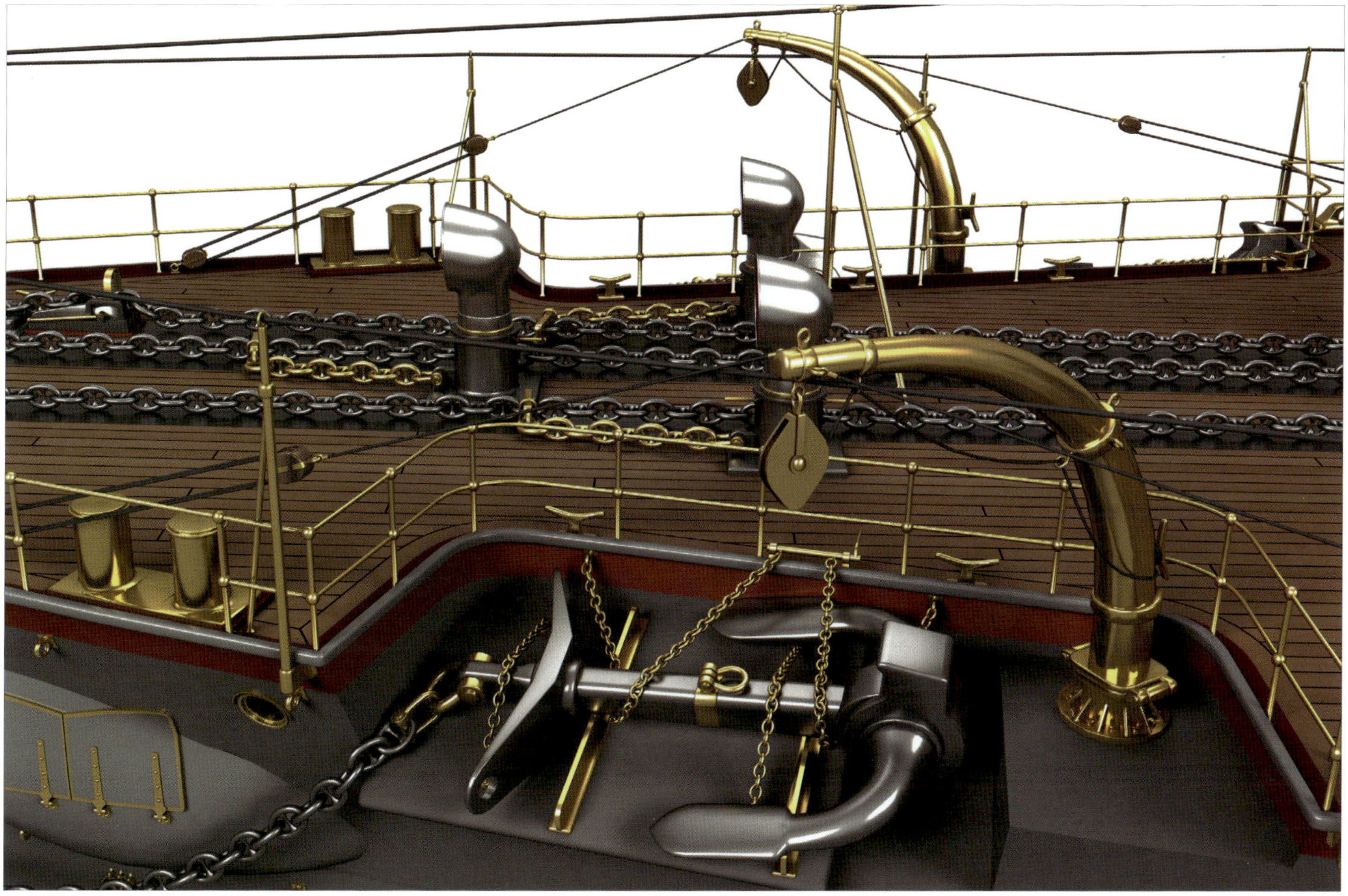

View of the anchors and crane beam, port side.

View of the chart room.

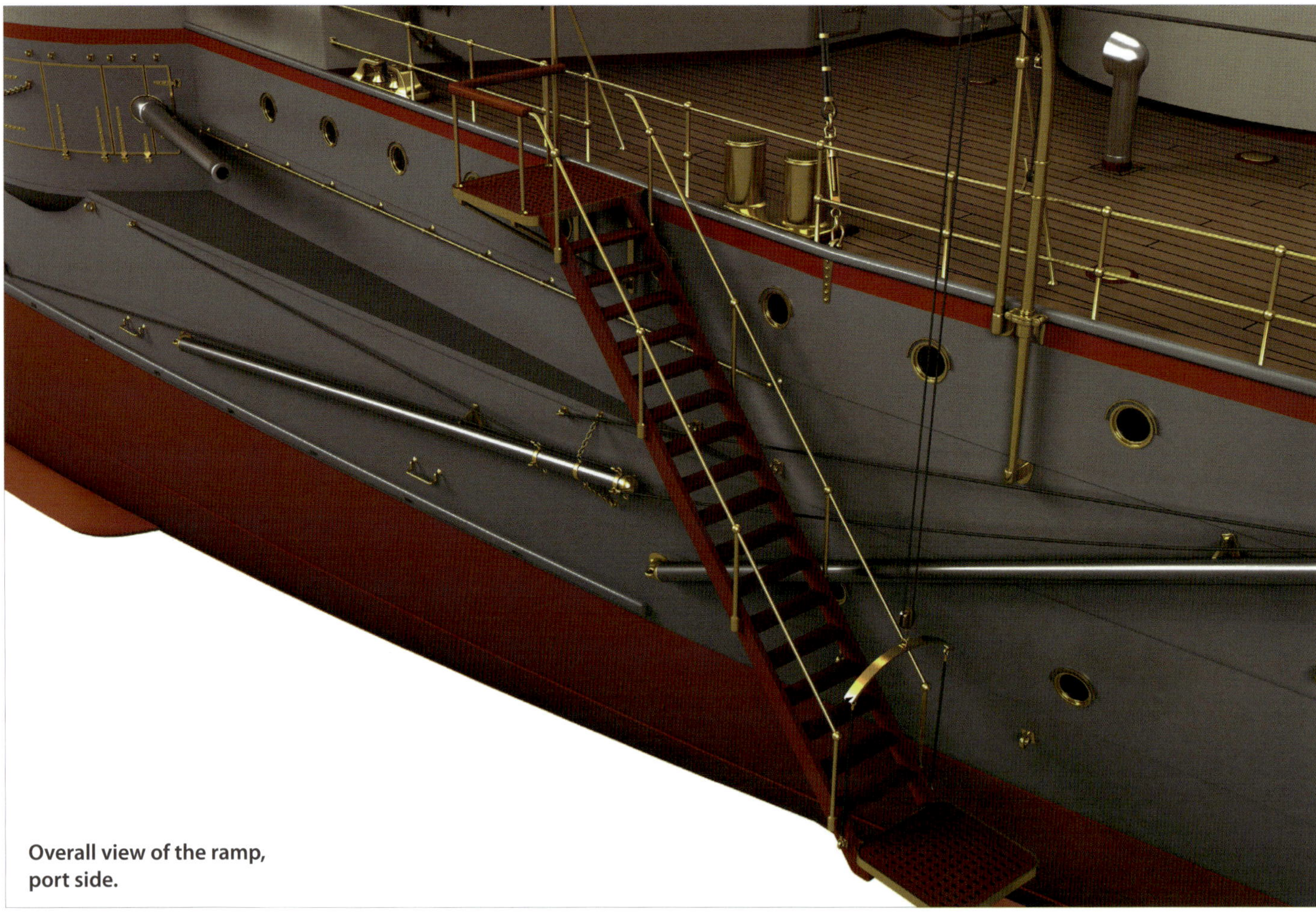

Overall view of the ramp, port side.

Close-up view of the central superstructure of the ship, port side.

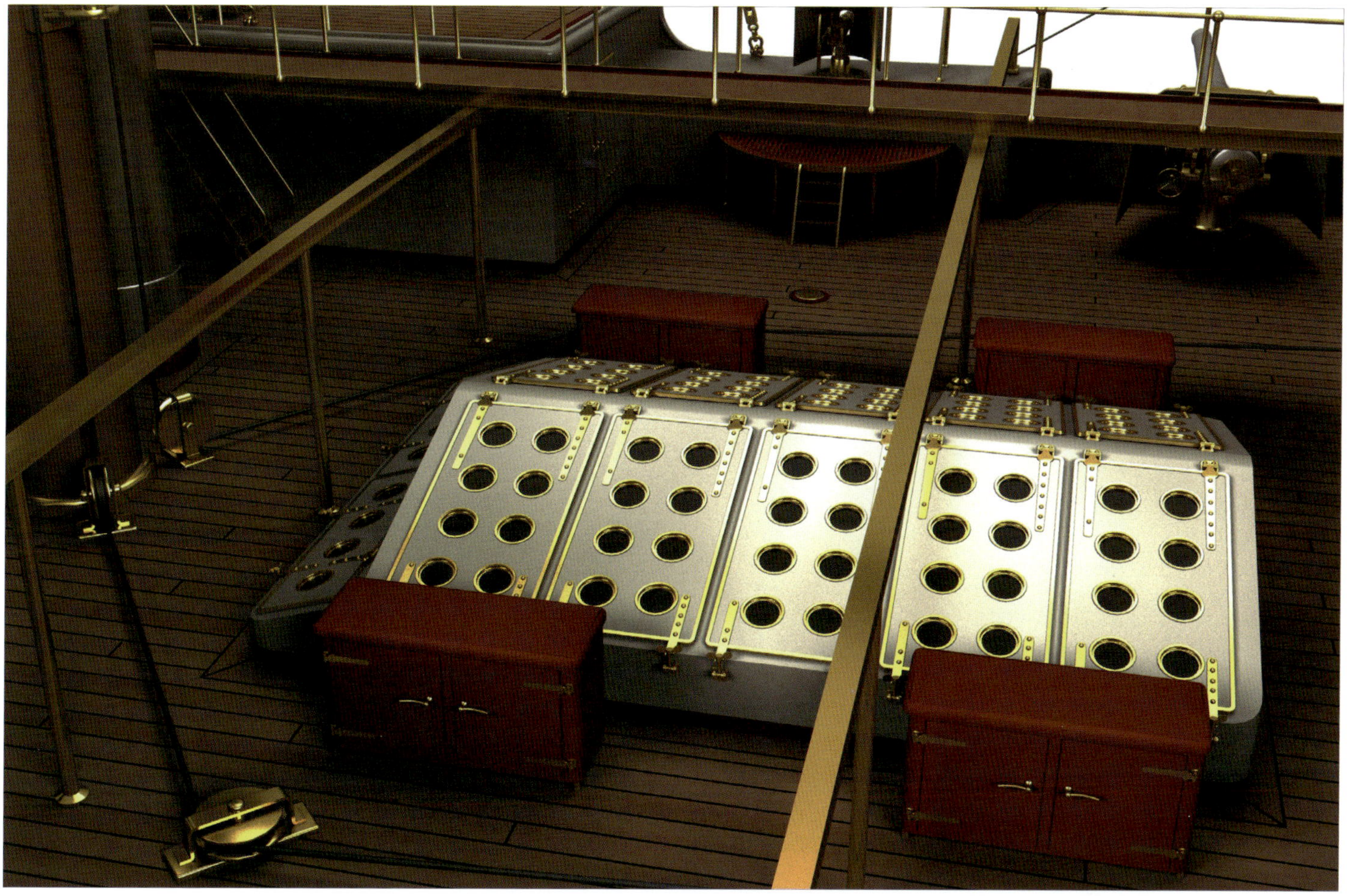

Close-up view of the cabin skylight.

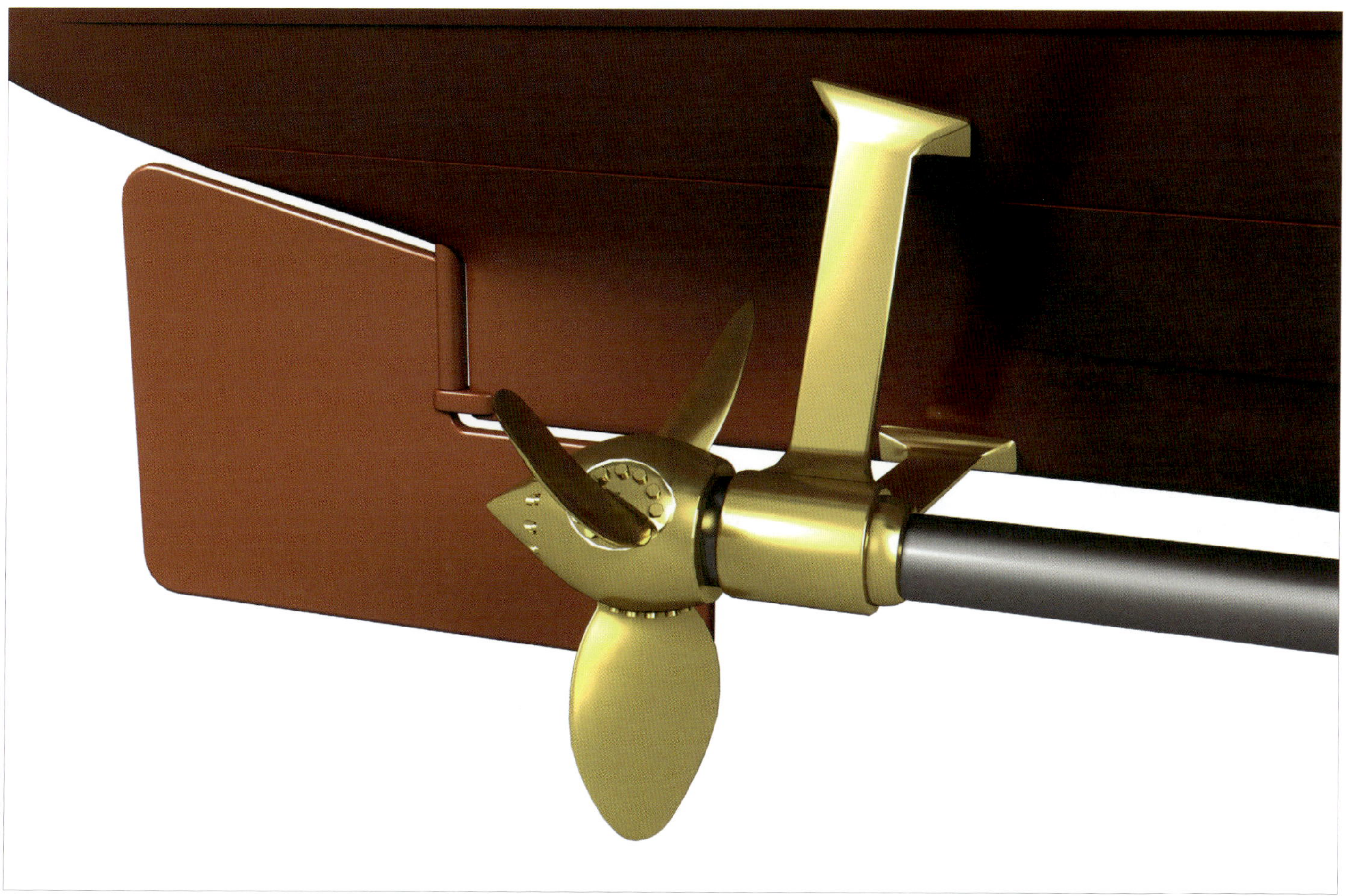

Close-up view of the propeller, starboard side.

Overall view of the ship.

Overall view of the ship, port side.

12-pounder 8 cwt Armstrong gun (landing gun).

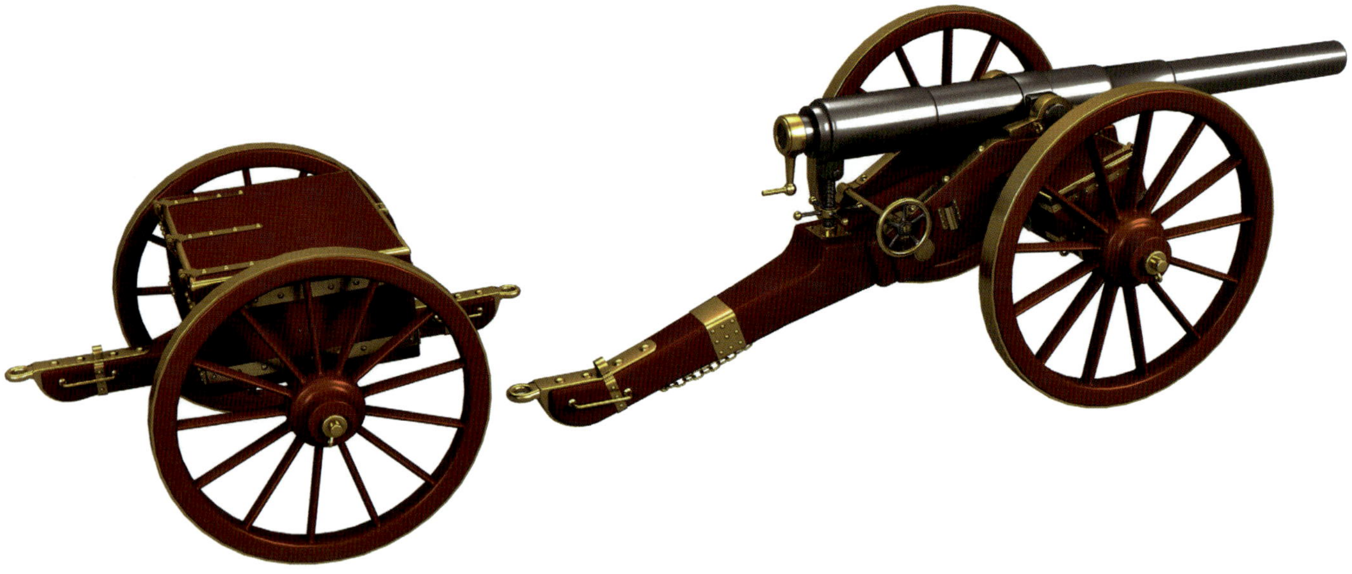

12-pounder 8 cwt Armstrong gun (landing gun).

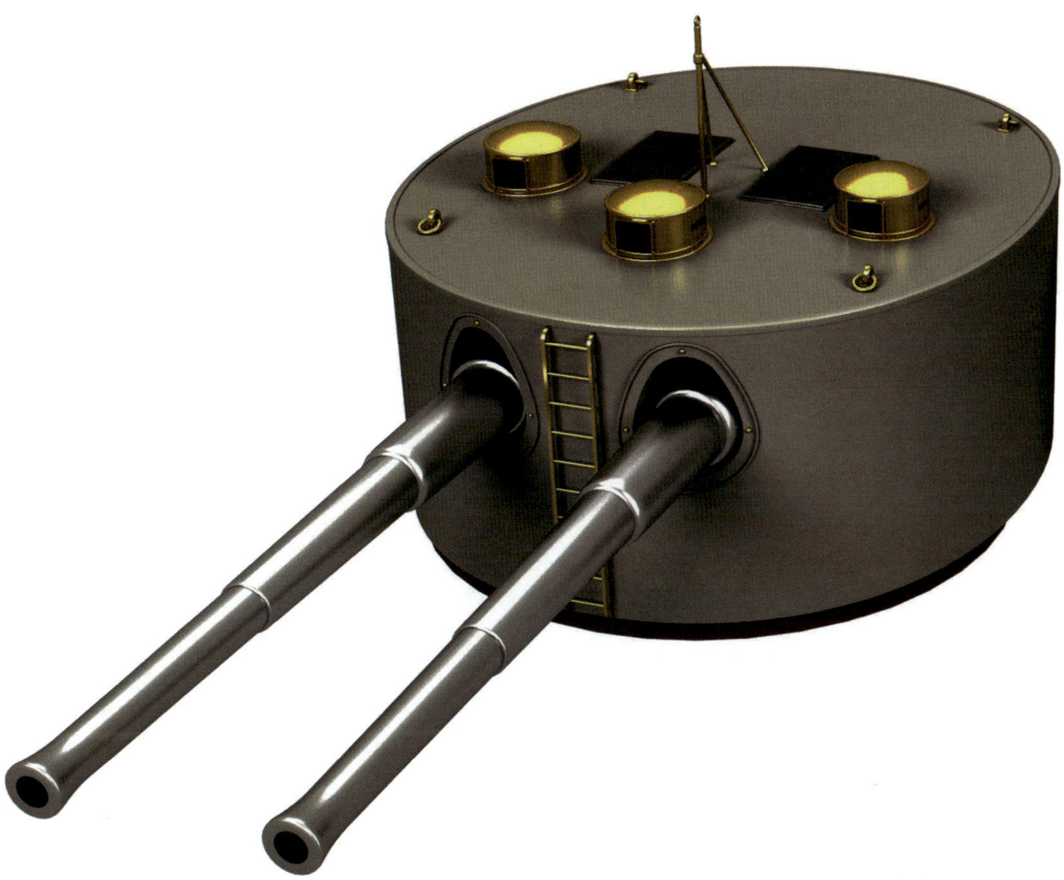

Turret of 8-inch guns.

Turret of 8-inch guns.

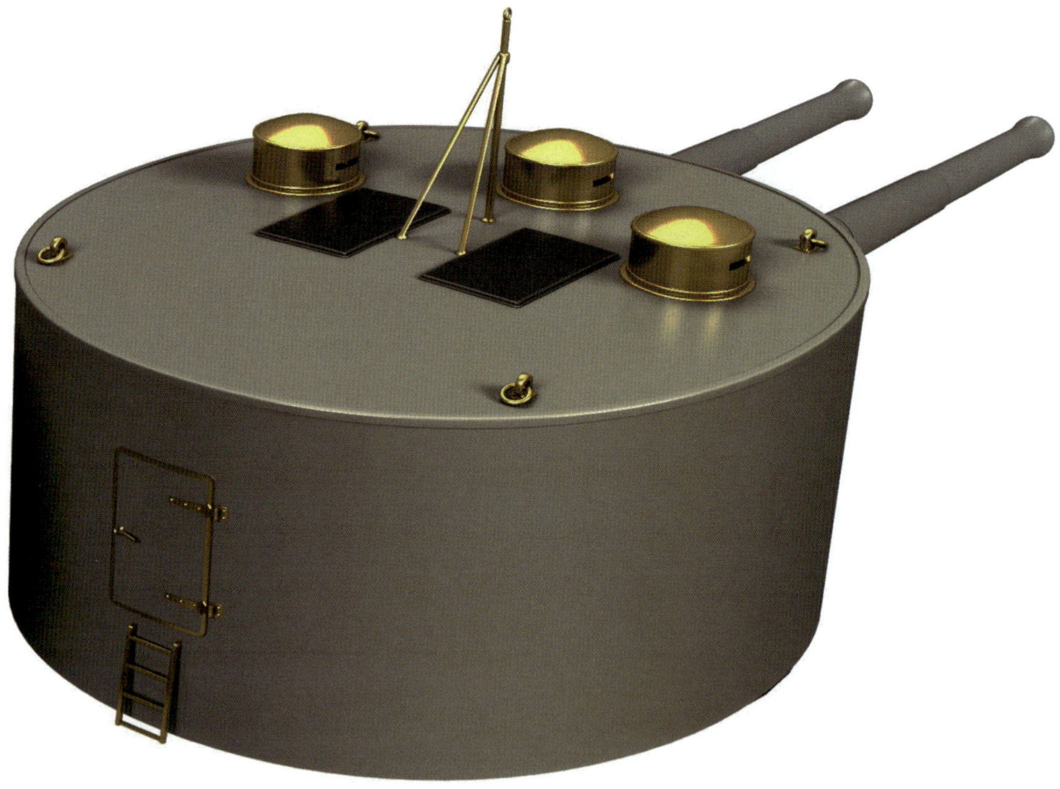

6-inch Armstrong gun, in the shield mount.

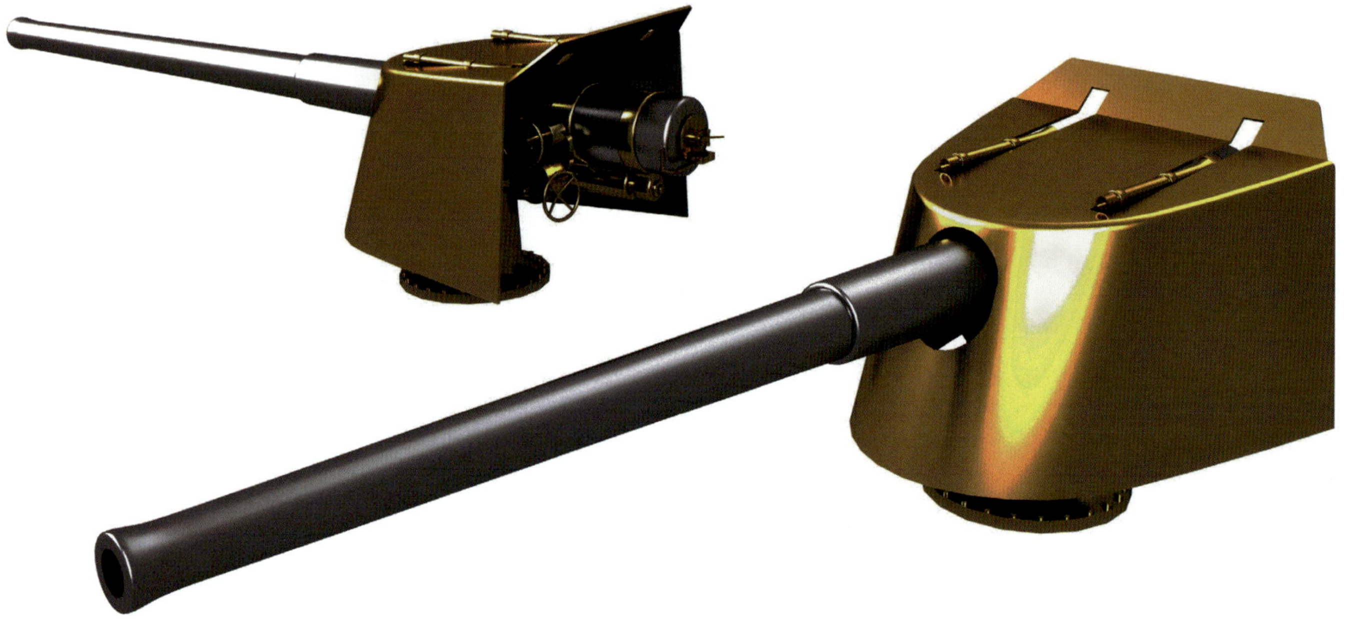

3-inch Armstrong gun, in the shield mount.

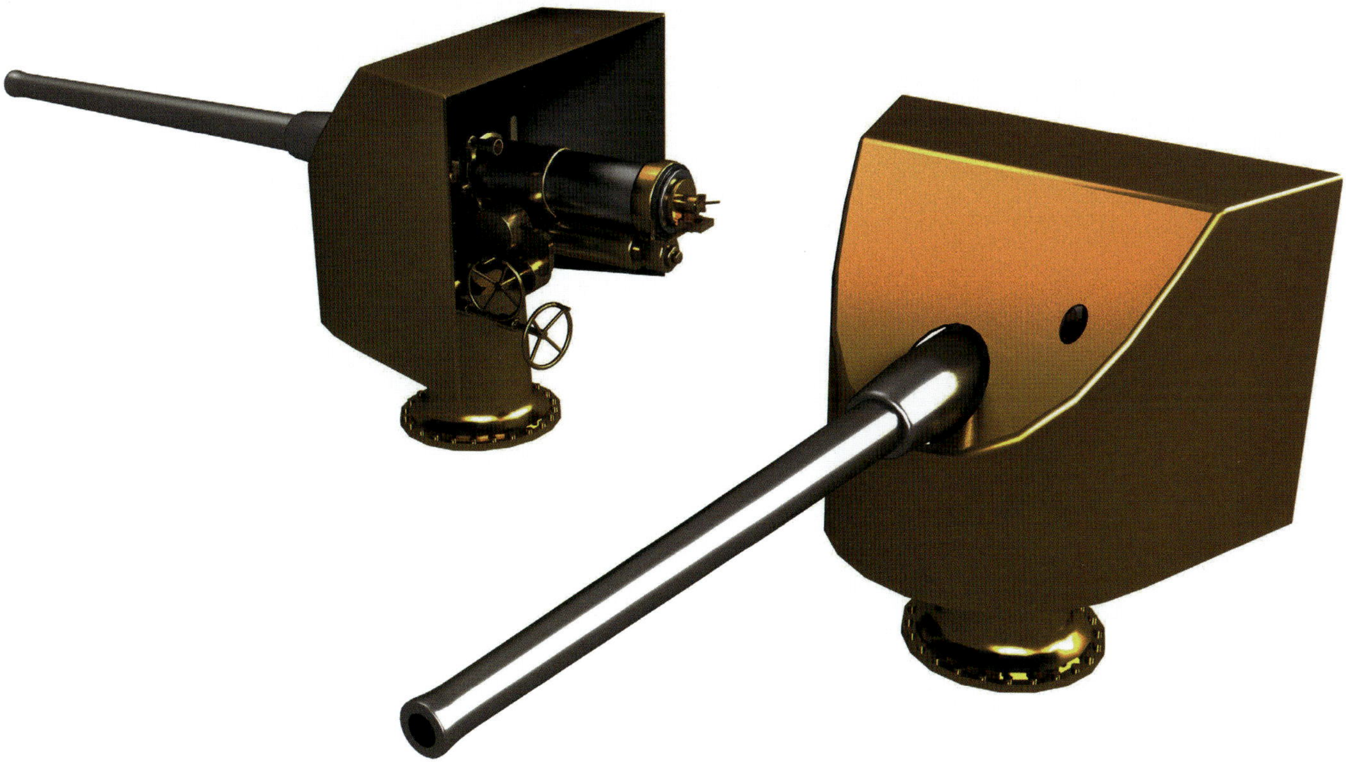

47 mm Hotchkiss gun in the shield mount.

Overall view of the ship, starboard side.

Overall view of the ship, starboard side.

The Japanese Cruiser Asama – Aliaksandr Sukhanevich

LUBLIN 2021 • ISBN 978-83-66673-44-1

3D illustrations and captions: **Aliaksandr Sukhanevich** • Text: **Jan Radziemski** • Text translation: **Stanisław Powała-Niedźwiecki** • Design: **KAGERO STUDIO** – Łukasz Maj

KAGERO Publishing • www.kagero.pl, e-mail: kagero@kagero.pl, marketing@kagero.pl

Editorial office, Marketing, Distribution: KAGERO Publishing, Akacjowa 100, os. Borek, Turka, 20-258 Lublin 62, Poland, phone/fax (+48) 81 501 21 05

www.kagero.eu

3D visualisations are based on the available photographs, drawings and other archive data, and should be treated only as author's attempt to recreate the original look of the particular machine as faithfully as possible. If you are in possession of materials to which author did not reach, and you would like to help us to develop a better publication, please contact the Publisher on: redakcja@kagero.pl